ideas

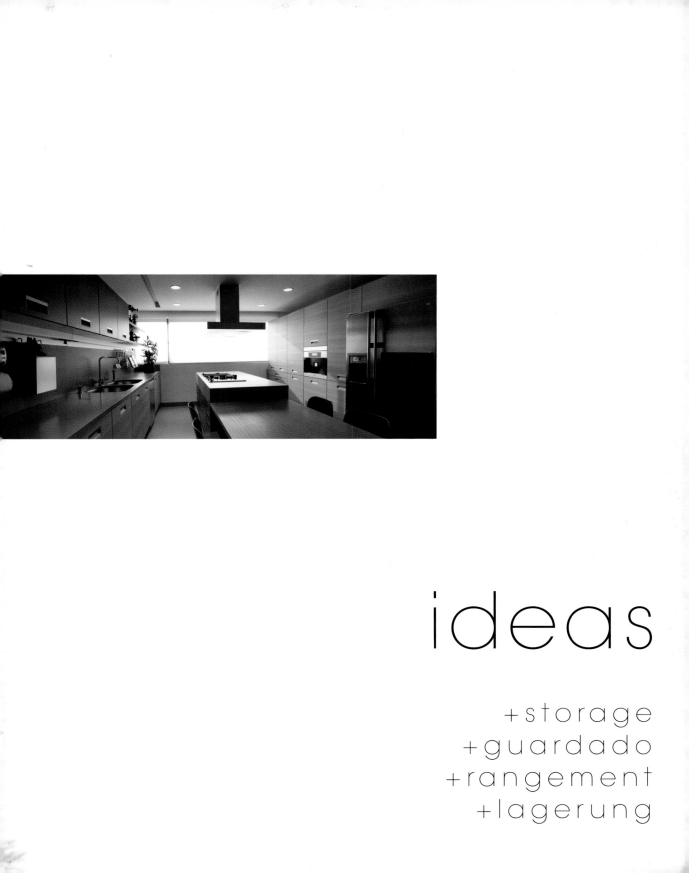

ideas

+storage
+guardado
+rangement
+lagerung

AUTHORS
Fernando de Haro & Omar Fuentes

EDITORIAL DESIGN & PRODUCTION

EDITORES

PROJECT MANAGERS
Edali Nuñez Daniel
Laura Mijares Castellá

COORDINATION
Laura Mar Hernández Morales

PREPRESS COORDINATION
Carolina Medina Granados

COPYWRITER
Roxana Villalobos

ENGLISH TRANSLATION
Babel International Translators

FRENCH TRANSLATION
Architextos: Translation Services and Language Solutions

GERMAN TRANSLATION
Angloamericano de Cuernavaca
Sabine Klein

Ideas
+storage . +guardado . +rangement . + lagerung

© 2011, Fernando de Haro & Omar Fuentes

AM Editores S.A. de C.V.
Paseo de Tamarindos 400 B, suite 109, Col. Bosques de las Lomas,
C.P. 05120, México, D.F., Tel. 52(55) 5258 0279
E-mail: ame@ameditores.com   www.ameditores.com

ISBN: 978-607-437-087-4

Printed in China.

introduction   introducción

Storage refers to keeping things in a given place. Every house has somewhere for storing food, tools, clothing, photos, medicines, books, documents, dishes, tablecloths, gardening implements, cutlery and wine, to mention just a few examples from an endless inventory.

Storage involves choosing a container that suits the type of objects to be stored and satisfies their specific needs for optimum preservation, as well as providing some form of order.

Le llamamos guardado a la función y acción de almacenar. En todas las casas existen áreas para almacenaje de comida, herramientas, ropa, fotografías, medicamentos, libros, papeles, vajillas, manteles, utensilios de jardín, cubiertos, vinos, por nombrar sólo algunos de entre un variado inventario.

Guardar implica elegir un contenedor de acuerdo con el tipo de objetos y las necesidades particulares que éstos demandan para su óptima preservación, así como organizar su acomodamiento.

introduction　　　einleitung

Appelés meubles de rangement, on les trouve dans tous les logements et ils sont logiquement conçus pour y garder toutes sortes de marchandises : aliments, outils, médicaments, livres, papiers, du vin, des couverts, de la vaisselle, du linge de table, des ustensiles de jardin … pour ne citer que quelques exemples.

Conserver des choses sous-entend que le meuble qui a cette fonction est conçu pour le faire dans des conditions optimales et pour offrir les solutions de rangement adéquates.

Lagerung ist die Funktion und die Aktion des Aufbewahrens. In allen Häusern gibt es Plätze zur Aufbewahrung von Lebensmitteln, Werkzeug, Kleidung, Fotos, Medikamenten, Büchern, Papieren, Geschirrs, Tischdecken, Gartengeräten, Besteckes, Wein, um nur einiges des umfangreichen Bestandes zu nennen.

Lagerung beinhaltet einen für die Sache angebrachten, die spezifischen Bedürfnisse für ihren optimalen Schutz erfüllenden, Behälter zu finden, sowie seine Unterbringung zu organisieren.

In other words, just having a space is not enough. It is also necessary to plan what is going to be stored and how, otherwise it is unlikely that we will make the most of the available area which will just become an unruly mess.

So what needs to be taken into account when it comes to designing places for storage? To begin with, we need to identify which items are going to be stored and what their characteristics are. Then the areas they will be stored in have to be defined. Afterwards, the furniture needs to be planned with great care to make sure it is both functional and practical, but without neglecting its shape, depth, height and of course look.

Modular furniture has become popular and is considered ideal for storage purposes thanks to its flexibility and simplicity. It either comprises sets of independent modules or relies on divisions with boards or panels made of the same material used to make the module itself. The number of things that can be stored

Es decir, no basta con tener el espacio, es importante planear lo que se guarda y cómo se guarda; si no, se corre el riesgo de desaprovechar un área útil y convertirla en un simple depósito sin control ni orden.

¿Qué es lo que se debe tener en cuenta a la hora de diseñar los sitios de guardado? En primer término es sustancial identificar los objetos que se van a acopiar y sus características, y definir las zonas que se ocuparán para guardar. Luego es necesario planificar los muebles cuidando que sean funcionales y prácticos, sin perder de vista su forma, profundidad, altura y, desde luego, su estética.

Por su flexibilidad y simplicidad geométrica, los modulares han ganado terreno y son considerados muebles óptimos para el almacenamiento. Se conforman ya sea por composiciones de módulos independientes o a través de divisiones que se hacen a cada uno de ellos con tablones o tableros del mismo material con el

La taille du meuble n'est donc pas le seul facteur qui compte; il faut également penser à ce qui va y être rangé et aux possibilités pour y parvenir. Si on ne le fait pas, le risque est grand de ne pas profiter de l'espace offert et d'en faire une simple réserve sans ordre particulier.

Que doit-on prendre en compte au moment où l'on pense aménager un espace de rangement? Il est d'abord essentiel de bien réfléchir aux objets à conserver, à leurs caractéristiques, puis de délimiter les zones où ils vont prendre place. Ensuite, il faut concevoir des meubles qui seront à la fois fonctionnels et pratiques sans oublier leur esthétique (forme) et leurs dimensions (profondeur, hauteur).

De géométrie simple et à usages multiples, les meubles modulaires ont récemment gagné en popularité. On estime d'ailleurs qu'ils sont tout indiqués pour y ranger des choses. On peut en associer plusieurs pour

Man kann sagen, dass es nicht ausreicht den Platz zu haben, es ist wichtig zu planen was man aufbewahren möchte und wie es aufbewahrt wird; wenn man das nicht macht, läuft man Gefahr nützlichen Platz zu verschwenden und ihn in ein schlichtes Depot ohne Kontrolle und Ordnung zu verwandeln.

Was sollte man bedenken, wenn man Stauräume entwirft? Als erstes ist es wesentlich die Objekte, die aufbewahrt werden sollen, und ihre Eigenschaften zu identifizieren und die Plätze zu bestimmen die als Stauraum genutzt werden sollen. Dann ist es notwendig die Möbel zu planen, sie sollten funktionell und praktisch sein, ohne dabei deren Form, Tiefe, Höhe und natürlich auch ihr Aussehen, aus den Augen zu verlieren.

Durch ihre Vielseitigkeit und geometrische Schlichtheit sind Modulelemente auf dem Vormarsch und sie werden als optimale Möbel für die Aufbewahrung betrachtet.

in this type of furniture varies depending on the number of shelves and compartments available.

Manufacturers of modular furniture have devised efficient systems offering flexible solutions that adapt easily to the space in question. They are also making furniture with novel, tough and easy-to-clean materials that require little maintenance and look great. This type of furniture is often used in libraries, living rooms, dressing rooms, bathrooms and kitchens.

Contemporary modular furniture provides some wonderful storage options, but it is not the only one. Storage also extends to work furniture, drawers, cupboards, console tables, certain items of classic furniture such as trunks and chests, and other lighter objects like shelves, ledges, coat racks, and even loose boxes, or more specialized locations such as cellars.

This book has been divided into four main chapters to make it easier to digest: living areas, kitchens and dining rooms, bedrooms and bathrooms, and auxiliary zones. It is packed with tips and suggestions for carrying out projects, simplifying storage and bringing order and harmony to the home.

Readers are presented with a whole array of options so they can choose the one that best suits them and the space they have. But this book also strongly encourages them to opt for an original, tailor-made design of their very own.

que está construido el propio módulo. La cantidad de cosas que se puede guardar en estos muebles es muy variable, y varía en función del número de estantes y compartimientos que tenga cada uno.

Los fabricantes de modulares han creado sistemas eficaces con los que ofrecen soluciones versátiles y relativamente fáciles de adecuar a cualquier contexto espacial. También han incorporado a su producción materiales novedosos, resistentes, sencillos de limpiar, de bajo mantenimiento y muy lucidores. La mayor aplicación de sus productos está en bibliotecas, salas de TV, vestidores, baños y cocinas.

Si bien los modulares contemporáneos implican una verdadera fuente de soluciones para el almacenaje, no representan la única opción para este aspecto central de la vida en el hogar. El guardado abarca también muebles de obra, cajoneras, trinchadores, consolas, algunos muebles clásicos como baúles y cofres, y otros ligeros del tipo de repisas, estantes, percheros, llegando hasta las cajas sueltas, o aquellos especializados como las cavas.

Para facilitar su consulta, este volumen está estructurado en cuatros capítulos básicos: zonas de estar, cocinas y comedores, recámaras y baños, y zonas auxiliares. Contiene ideas y propuestas para concretar proyectos, simplificar el almacenaje y conseguir orden y armonía en la casa.

Hay un cúmulo de opciones para que sea el propio lector quien analice cuál es la alternativa que más le conviene o la que más oportuna resulta para su espacio; pero el libro también es una invitación para que se anime por un diseño a medida, propio y original.

former un tout ou, au contraire, les diviser par le biais de panneaux, de tablettes fabriqués dans le même matériau que celui des meubles. Le volume de choses que l'on peut conserver dans ce genre de mobilier est variable car tout dépend du nombre d'étagères et de compartiments disponibles.

Les fabricants de ce type de meubles ont mis au point des systèmes efficaces pour que le consommateur dispose de multiples solutions afin de les adapter aisément à son logement. Ces fabricants utilisent de même des matériaux innovants, résistants, simples à entretenir et à nettoyer et qui sont agréables à l'œil. On trouve principalement ces meubles dans les espaces pour lire, les salons télé, dressings, salles de bain et cuisines.

Bien que les meubles modulaires offrent un très grand nombre de solutions pour conserver des choses, ce ne sont pas les seuls qui répondent à cette fonction essentielle dans un logement. Car parmi les meubles de rangement, on peut également mentionner ceux qui font partie de la construction, les armoires à multiples placards, les buffets, les consoles. Certains sont de facture classique comme les malles et les coffres, d'autres sont plus légers comme les étagères, les patères, voire même des boîtes superposées ou des caves à vin.

Pour en faciliter la lecture, cet ouvrage est divisé en quatre chapitres : pièces de vie, cuisines et salles à manger, chambres et salles de bain, espaces secondaires et on y trouve des idées, des propositions afin de concrétiser certains projets, de simplifier le rangement, d'ordonner et d'arranger la maison.

Les options proposées sont multiples et le lecteur pourra choisir celle qui lui convient bien ou celle qui répond au mieux à son logement. Mais ce livre l'incitera avant tout à inventer son propre design original.

Sie bestehen aus Sets unabhängiger Möbel oder werden durch Platten oder Regalbrettern des gleichen Materials miteinander verbunden, um ein eigenes Modul zu formen. Die Menge, die in diesen Möbeln verstaut werden kann, ist sehr unterschiedlich, und hängt von der Anzahl der Zwischenböden und Fächern jedes einzelnen ab.

Die Hersteller von Modulmöbeln haben effiziente Systeme geschaffen mit denen sie vielfälltige Lösungen anbieten, die sich relativ leicht an die jeweiligen räumlichen Gegebenheiten anpassen lassen. Sie haben auch neue, widerstandsfähige, einfach zu reinigende, geringe Pflege erfordernde und sehr schöne Materialien in ihre Produktion aufgenommen. Ihre Produkte finden am häufigsten in Bibliotheken, Fensehräumen, Ankleidezimmern, Badezimmern und Küchen Anwendung.

Wenn auch die zeitgenössischen Module eine wirkliche Quelle für Lösungen bei der Aufbewahrung sind, sind sie nicht die einzige Option für diesen zentralen Bereich des häuslichen Lebens. Lagerung umfasst auch massgefertigte Möbel, Kommoden, Anrichten, Konsolen, einige klassische Möbel wie Truhen und andere leichte, wie Borde, Regale, Garderoben, bis zu einzelnen Kästen oder sehr speziellen wie Weinregalen.

Um das Nachschlagen zu erleichtern, ist dieser Band in vier Hauptkapitel unterteilt: Wohnräume, Küchen und Esszimmer, Schlafzimmer und Badezimmer, und sonstige Bereiche. Er enthält Ideen und Vorschläge um Projekte umzusetzen, die Aufbewahrung zu erleichtern und Ordnung und Harmonie im Haus zu schaffen.

Es gibt eine Vielzahl von Optionen, damit der Leser selbst analysiert, welche die für ihn am günstigste Alternative ist oder welche am besten zu den räumlichen Gegebenheiten passt; aber das Buch ist auch eine Einladung sich zu einem massgefertigem Design, einzigartig und originell, anzuregen zu lassen.

living areas

zonas de estar

pièces de vie

wohnräume

THE ROLE ENTRUSTED TO THE STUDY involves storing everything required for working at home. Bookshelves, a table or desk and a comfy chair are all essential. Some studies also need a TV set or stereo, so assigning them a specific location is a good idea. Leaving a space uninterrupted and covered between shelves for hanging a painting or framed photo is a great decorative option.

LA VOCACIÓN DE LOS ESTUDIOS es alojar todo lo necesario para trabajar en casa. Una estantería, una mesa o un escritorio y una cómoda silla son sus elementos básicos. Algunos despachos requieren también incorporar televisores o equipos de sonido, por lo que es conveniente asignar un sitio para colocarlos. Una alternativa decorativa consiste en dejar entre los anaqueles una parte sólida y tapada, que sirva para colgar un cuadro.

UN BUREAU est conçu pour abriter tout ce qui est nécessaire au travail à la maison. Le mobilier de base est constitué par des étagères, une table ou un bureau auquel on ajoutera une chaise confortable. Mais certains espaces de travail doivent être équipés d'une télévision, d'une chaîne stéréo. Il est donc important de prévoir des endroits à cet effet. Pour y parvenir, on peut, par exemple, aménager un compartiment solide et fermé dans un meuble à étagères et y accrocher un tableau.

STUDIOS BEHERBERGEN alles Notwendige um zu Hause zu arbeiten. Regale, ein Tisch oder ein Schreibtisch und ein bequemer Stuhl sind die Grundausstattung. Einige Büros benötigen auch einen Fernseher oder eine Stereoanlage, weswegen es einen Platz für sie geben sollte. Eine Alternative in der Dekoration besteht daraus, zwischen den Wandregalen eine Abdeckung anzubringen, um ein Bild aufzuhängen.

studies estudios bureaux arbeitsräume

The lower sections of shelves can be used as wide, deep drawers, which are very useful for storing all types of objects and accessories inherent to a study.

Es factible aprovechar las zonas bajas de los estantes para crear cajoneras de buenos anchos y profundidad, éstas son muy útiles para almacenar todo tipo de accesorios inherentes a un estudio.

Le bas d'un meuble à étagères peut facilement être modifié pour contenir des tiroirs larges et profonds très utiles pour y ranger toute sorte d'accessoires propres à un bureau.

Es ist möglich, die unteren Teile der Regale zu nutzen um Schubladen guter Breite und Tiefe zu schaffen, die sehr nützlich sind, um all die einem Studio eigenen Sachen aufzubewahren.

A good way to make the most of the available space is to use the entire height and width of a wall to embed an item of furniture comprising bookshelves, desks and drawers.

Una excelente idea para hacer rendir el área es destinar la altura y anchura totales de un muro y empotrar a éste un mueble en el que se integre librero, escritorios y cajoneras.

Pour profiter au maximum de la hauteur et de la largeur d'un mur, il est possible d'y encastrer un très grand meuble qui comprendra une bibliothèque, des bureaux et des tiroirs.

Es ist eine hervorragende Idee den vorhandenen Platz vollständig auszunutzen und die gesamte Höhe und Breite einer Wand für ein Möbel zu nutzen, in dem Bücherregal, Schreibtische und Schubladen eingebaut sind.

ONE WAY OF TONING DOWN THE SQUARENESS of these shelves is to divide them into two sections of different sizes using a focal component, such as a picture, and leaving niches also of different sizes to hold books or works of art. This solution transforms a conventional item of furniture into a highly decorative creation.

PARA ROMPER CON LA CUADRATURA de la estantería se puede optar por dividirla en dos secciones de distintas dimensiones a partir de un elemento focal, que bien puede ser un cuadro; y dejar nichos de diversas proporciones para acomodar tanto libros como piezas de arte. Con esta solución se transforma un mueble convencional en un elemento con un alto valor decorativo.

GRÂCE À UN ÉLÉMENT QUI ATTIRE LE REGARD (un tableau, par exemple), il est possible de diviser la forme rectangulaire d'un meuble à étagères en deux parties distinctes et d'y laisser des vides de dimensions variées pour y mettre des livres ou des objets d'art. Le meuble, de forme conventionnelle, constitue alors une véritable réussite artistique.

UM MIT DER QUADRATISCHEN FORM eines Regales zu brechen, kann man es, mit etwas Auffälligem - das gut ein Gemälde sein kann - in zwei Stücke verschiedener Grösse unterteilen und Nischen verschiedener Ausmasse lassen, um sowohl Bücher als auch Kunstgegenstände unterzubringen. Mit dieser Lösung verwandelt man ein konventionelles Möbel in ein Element mit hohem dekorativem Wert.

A CAREFUL ARRANGEMENT OF VOLUMES in shelves will make a real contribution to the room. This is why it is better not to overload them and just allow them to look good, combining their esthetic and practical qualities. Shelves consisting of modules of identical sizes bestow a sense of balance to the ambience, while different sized modules make for greater vibrancy.

EL BUEN ACOMODO DE LOS VOLÚMENES en los anaqueles significa una aportación para la habitación. Por ello, en ocasiones conviene no saturarlos y dejar que luzca el mueble combinando estética y funcionalidad. Aquellos estantes diseñados por módulos de dimensiones idénticas hacen que el área se sienta equilibrada, en tanto que los de distintas dimensiones generan un espacio dinámico.

SAVOIR RANGER SES LIVRES SUR DES étagères est un plus dans la décoration d'une chambre. Il ne faut pas trop saturer le meuble et trouver le bon équilibre entre esthétique et côté pratique. Avec une bibliothèque composée de modules de dimensions identiques, l'espace est équilibré. Avec des modules de dimensions variées, l'espace se caractérisera, cette fois, par son dynamisme.

EINE GESCHICKTE ANORDNUNG DER BÜCHER IN DEN REGALEN ist ein Beitrag zur Dekoration des Raumes. Deshalb ist es manchmal besser sie nicht zu überladen und das Möbelstück selbst durch die Verbindung von Ästhetik und Funktionalität wirken zu lassen. Regale, die als Module in gleicher Grösse entworfen sind, lassen den Bereich ausgewogen erscheinen, während verschiedene Grössen den Raum dynamisch wirken lassen.

SHELVES WITH DOORS on the front offer a great means of protecting books and other objects from dust. A more stylish touch can be provided with the inclusion of a fireplace and by completing the décor with a few shelves housing sculptures, vases and other items that lend their weight to the room's vitality and warmth.

UNA FORMA MUY PRÁCTICA de mantener los libros y otros objetos resguardados del polvo es cubrir los estantes con puertas delanteras. Adicionalmente, para crear un ambiente con estilo se puede incluir una chimenea y completar la decoración con algunas repisas que sirvan para ubicar esculturas, floreros y otros elementos que le brinden una mayor vitalidad y calidez a la zona.

LORSQUE L'ON SOUHAITE protéger les livres et d'autres objets de la poussière, il suffit de couvrir les étagères par des portes s'ouvrant vers l'extérieur. Pour doter la pièce d'un certain style, on peut, en plus, y ajouter une cheminée et terminer la décoration avec quelques étagères sur lesquelles prendront place des sculptures, vases et autres éléments qui apportent un peu de vitalité et de chaleur dans l'espace.

EINE PRAKTISCHE Weise Bücher und andere Objekte staubfrei zu halten, ist es, die Regale mit Türen zu versehen. Zusätzlich kann man, um ein stilvolles Ambiente zu erzielen, einen Kamin einbauen und die Dekoration mit einigen Regalbrettern ergänzen, auf denen man Skulpturen, Vasen und andere Elemente, die mehr Leben und Wärme in den Bereich einführen, stellen kann.

IF DOCUMENTS NEED TO BE KEPT, as well as books, filing cabinets with ring-bound or clip folders are the best bet. In order to ensure uniformity, they should all be the same size and have the same finish. Tags and identifiers attached to the sides will help classify documents.

CUANDO NO SÓLO se requiere guardar libros, sino también conservar documentos, los muebles archiveros con múltiples cajoneras, así como las carpetas archivadoras con argollas o con pinza sujetapapeles son ideales. Para dar la sensación de uniformidad es importante que estas últimas tengan el mismo tamaño y acabado en sus cubiertas. Ayudan a la clasificación los identificadores y etiquetas colocados en los lomos.

SI L'ON SOUHAITE conserver des livres mais aussi des documents, les meubles pour archives avec leurs tiroirs multiples sont foncièrement recommandés tout comme les classeurs munis d'anneaux ou de pinces. Afin d'uniformiser le tout, il est important que les classeurs soient tous de la même taille et du même matériau. Et avec des étiquettes et autres indications sur la tranche, ranger les documents sera plus facile.

WENN MAN NICHT NUR Bücher, sondern auch Akten unterbringen muss, sind Aktenschränke mit mehreren Schubladen, Aktenrordner mit Ringen oder mit Papierklammern ideal. Um den Eindruck von Einheitlichkeit zu bewahren, sollten letztere die gleiche Grösse und das gleiche Aussehen haben. Bei der Einordnung helfen Etiketten auf den Rücken der Ordner.

THE MOST VERSATILE PART OF THE HOME is the TV room. Its design should be functional and practical, and in accordance with the activities that take place there. Apart from being a place for watching TV, it is also where people listen to music, chat with friends, engage in leisure activities and receive visitors. Be it as it may, the focal point of this room is the furniture housing the TV, around which the rest of the furniture will be arranged.

LA SALA DE TELEVISIÓN es el área más versátil de la casa. Su diseño debe ser funcional, práctico y responder a las actividades que se realicen en ella. Por lo común se usa, además de para ver televisión, para escuchar música, charlar con amigos, llevar a cabo actividades recreativas o recibir visitas… Como sea, el punto focal en esta zona es el mueble de TV, y en torno a éste se distribuye el resto del mobiliario.

LE SALON POUR VOIR LA TÉLÉVISION est la pièce à qui l'on attribue le plus grand nombre de fonctions. Son design doit donc être fonctionnel, pratique et conçu pour toutes les activités qui y prendront place. On y regarde la télé certes, mais on y écoute aussi de la musique, on discute avec des amis, on se distrait, on reçoit … Le meuble de la télé occupe bien évidemment l'endroit le plus visible et le reste du mobilier prend place autour.

DAS FERNSEHZIMMER ist das am vielseitigsten benutzte im Haus. Sein Design muss funktionell sein, praktisch und den Aktivitäten entsprechen, die in ihm ausgeführt werden. Normalerweise wird in ihm, ausser fernzusehen, Musik gehört, sich mit Freunden unterhalten, seinen Hobbies nachgegangen oder Besuch empfangen … wie dem auch sei, die Hauptsache in ihm ist das Fernsehmöbel, und um es herum werden die restlichen Möbelstücke angeordnet.

tv rooms
salas de televisión
salons télé
fernsehzimmer

A TV ROOM is often where ornaments of a more personal nature are placed, including family or personal photos, and other favorite objects. Attention needs to be paid to just how the furniture is modulated, and which material it is made from. Wood is an especially good option for its look, particularly the way it has been cut or carved and its texture.

UNA SALA DE TV se presta para introducir elementos decorativos con significación personal, como es el caso de fotografías familiares, personales y objetos favoritos, entre otros. Desde luego, es relevante la manera en la que se modula el mueble, así como el material del que está hecho. Particularmente la madera se presta a un trabajo lucidor, destacando las tallas y los texturizados.

LE SALON TÉLÉ est une pièce idéale pour y placer des éléments décoratifs dont l'importance est personnelle (photographies de la famille, des amis, objets favoris). La forme du meuble central et son matériau de fabrication y sont évidemment primordiaux. Le bois met en valeur le travail réalisé, en particulier la taille et les finitions du meuble.

EIN FERNSEHZIMMER bietet sich an, Dekorationsstücke mit persönlichem Wert aufzustellen, wie z.B. Fotografien der Familie, Objekte mit persönlicher Bedeutung, oder die einem besonders gefallen. Selbstverständlich ist die Form des Möbels und das Material aus dem es hergestellt wurde, wichtig. Besonders Holz bietet sich für eine hervorragende Verarbeitung an, dessen Muster und Textur betonend.

Multi-functional furniture helps maintain order in smaller spaces. The lower section of a table, for instance, can be used for storing books, while the TV stand can be fitted with drawers, and sofas can double up as beds with storage space.

Los muebles multifuncionales ayudan a mantener orden en espacios reducidos. Por ejemplo, la parte inferior de una mesa puede ser librero, el televisor tener delante unas cajoneras, y los sofás ser camas y contar con espacio de guardado.

Les meubles multifonctions contribuent à maintenir un certain ordre dans les pièces de petite taille. Le bas de la partie avant d'une table, par exemple, peut être doté de tiroirs et les canapés-lits peuvent être équipés d'espaces de rangement.

Multifunktionelle Möbel helfen in kleinen Räumen Ordnung zu halten. Zum Beispiel kann der untere Teil eines Tisches als Bücherregal dienen, der Fernseher hat unter sich einige Schubladen und die Sofas lassen sich in Betten verwandeln und verfügen über einen Stauraum.

THE HOME'S ENTERTAINMENT CENTER is increasingly also where communication mediums are located. Here a highly practical design that can house all the different items of equipment consists of drawers below and open modules above, leaving the space in between for the TV and a desk for the computer. The work zone is best served by having its very own light from a source attached to the shelves.

ES CADA VEZ MÁS COMÚN que el centro de entretenimiento se convierta en un núcleo de medios de comunicación. Un diseño muy práctico para alojar todos los equipos es con cajones inferiores y módulos abiertos superiores, dejando el espacio intermedio para acomodar la TV y para acondicionar un escritorio para la computadora. Es ideal que la zona de trabajo cuente con iluminación propia empotrada al estante.

LES PIÈCES POUR SE DÉTENDRE deviennent de plus en plus des endroits dédiés aux nouvelles technologies de la communication. Des tiroirs dans la partie inférieure du meuble principal et des espaces ouverts en haut sont indiqués pour y placer l'équipement. Au milieu, on placera la télévision et le bureau pour l'ordinateur. Et un éclairage encastré dans le meuble spécialement conçu pour l'espace de travail est idéal.

ES WIRD IMMER ÜBLICHER, dass sich das Zentrum der Unterhaltung in ein Herzstück der Kommunikation verwandelt. Ein praktisches Design, um alle Apparate unterzubringen, ist eins mit Schubladen in den unteren Bereichen und offenen Flächen oben, den mittleren Teil offen lassend, um den Fernsehapparat unterzubringen und einen Fläche für den Computer zu haben. Ideal ist es, dass der Arbeitsbereich über eine eigene, in die Regale eingebaute, Beleuchtung verfügt.

FLAT SCREENS have transformed TV furniture, as sets can now be embedded into the wall and still look great. One way to make the most of this possibility is with a raised shelf, independent of the TV, that neither touches the floor nor obstructs the space. Or it could be placed on top of a stand and raised a few centimeters above the floor.

LAS PANTALLAS PLANAS han dado un giro al mobiliario de televisión, pues se pueden instalar directamente sobre el muro y, dada su estética, quedar visibles. Aprovechando esta ventaja, es factible optar por una estantería volada, independiente de la TV, que no toque el piso y no estorbe en el camino, o bien hacerla reposar sobre un templete elevándola unos centímetros del suelo.

LES ÉCRANS PLATS ont profondément modifié les meubles télé. Il est dorénavant possible d'installer le téléviseur directement contre le mur. Objet esthétique, il n'est plus nécessaire de le dissimuler. On peut donc aménager une bibliothèque contre le mur qui ne repose pas sur le sol et qui ne gêne pas la circulation. Il est aussi possible de placer la télé sur un petit meuble à quelques centimètres du sol.

FLACHBILDSCHIRME haben die Fernsehmöbel verändert, da sie direkt an der Wand angebracht werden können und durch ihre Ästhetik sichtbar bleiben können. Diesen Vorteil nutzend, ist es möglich freihängende Regale zu wählen, unabhängig vom Fernseher, die nicht bis zum Boden reichen und Wege versperren oder sie auf einem Sockel anzubringen und sie damit einige Zentimeter über dem Boden zu platzieren.

bookshelves
libreros
bibliothèques
bücherregale

FROM A STORAGE POINT OF VIEW, the purpose of bookshelves is to keep books, which is why they perform such an important role. It should be borne in mind that, in their pursuit of originality, publishers produce books in all shapes and sizes. When it comes to designing bookshelves, it is always advisable to make sure dividing panels are located at different heights and are flexible in terms of width.

DESDE LA ÓPTICA DEL GUARDADO, la finalidad de las bibliotecas es recibir libros; por esta razón, el librero se convierte en su pieza fundamental. Conviene considerar el hecho de que, en un afán de originalidad, la industrial editorial produce libros de los tamaños más disímbolos; por ello, al planear el diseño del librero se aconseja dejar los entrepaños divisorios a distintas alturas y con anchos flexibles.

EN TANT QUE PIÈCES DE RANGEMENT, les salons-bibliothèques sont d'abord conçus pour contenir des livres. Le meuble de la bibliothèque en est donc le principal élément. Or, le marché du livre offre des ouvrages de formes et de tailles originales. En conséquence, il faut bien réfléchir au design de ce meuble en prévoyant des cloisons séparatrices de diverses hauteurs et largeurs.

AUS DER SICHT DER LAGERUNG ist es Aufgabe einer Bibliothek Bücher unterzubringen; darum wird das Regal zu ihrem Hauptelement. Man sollte berücksichtigen, dass die Verlage in dem Bemühen Originalität zu zeigen, Bücher in den verschiedensten Grössen produzieren; daher sollten die Fächer des Bücherregales in unterschiedlicher Breite und Höhe geplant werden.

MOST OF A ROOM'S VISUAL SPACE is taken up by walls and windows. Windows are usually left uncovered so that light can pour in freely. However, if the windows are large and there is plenty of light, a small part can be used, either at the top or at the bottom, to build made-to-measure shelves and create a storage area. This is an audacious move, but it provides splendid results.

LOS MUROS Y LAS VENTANAS ocupan la mayor parte del espacio visual de una habitación. Es común que se evite cubrir los ventanales para no interrumpir el paso de la luz. Sin embargo, cuando éstos son amplios y la iluminación es abundante, se puede emplear un fragmento, ya sea superior o inferior, para construir un librero a medida y conseguir área de guardado. Si bien la solución es atrevida, el efecto es sobresaliente.

LES MURS ET LES FENÊTRES occupent la plus grande partie de l'espace visuel d'une chambre. En général, les baies vitrées n'y sont pas couvertes pour laisser circuler la lumière. Mais lorsque ces dernières sont trop grandes et quand l'espace est trop éclairé, on peut décider d'en recouvrir une partie (supérieure ou inferieure) avec un espace de rangement sur mesure comme une bibliothèque. Cette solution est peut-être audacieuse mais l'effet produit est remarquable.

WÄNDE UND FENSTER nehmen den grössten Teil des optischen Raumes eines Zimmers ein. Üblicherweise vermeidet man die Fenster zu verdecken, um den Lichteinfall nicht zu stören. Allerdings kann man, wenn sie gross genug sind und der Raum sehr hell ist, einen Teil, sei es der Obere oder der Untere, nutzen, um ein massgefertigtes Regal anzubringen und somit Stauraum zu schaffen. Auch wenn diese Lösung gewagt scheint, ist das Ergebnis herausragend.

Steps perform a decorative role and are very practical in libraries if they are floor to ceiling, because they bring the higher shelves within reach. Greater stability can be achieved by including hand grips.

Las escaleras son elementos de decoración y muy prácticos en las bibliotecas de piso a techo, pues permiten alcanzar los estantes que se encuentran en niveles superiores. Para conseguir estabilidad conviene que tengan apoyos para las manos.

Les échelles sont des éléments autant décoratifs que pratiques pour les bibliothèques qui vont du sol au plafond. Elles permettent d'atteindre les étagères les plus élevées. Et pour qu'elles soient stables, des appuis pour les mains sont conseillés.

Leitern sind Elemente der Dekoration und sehr praktisch bei Regalen, die vom Boden bis zur Decke reichen, da sie erlauben an die Fächer in den oberen Bereichen zu gelangen. Um grössere Stabilität zu erreichen sollten sie Handläufe haben.

MODULAR SHELVES can come complete or pre-packaged to be assembled at home. The latter consists of panels of the same size that are put together until a functional item of furniture is obtained. Segments can also be extended in accordance with needs as they arise in order to provide a specific solution for a given space.

LOS ESTANTES MODULARES pueden ser de obra o venir pre-armados para ser ensamblados en casa. Estos últimos se componen por paneles de dimensiones idénticas que se van articulando entre sí, hasta conformar un mueble funcional. Además, ofrecen la posibilidad de ir ampliando segmentos de acuerdo con las necesidades que se van presentando y responder específicamente a un espacio.

LES ÉTAGÈRES MODULAIRES peuvent être vendues déjà montées ou sous forme d'éléments que l'on assemble chez soi. Dans ce dernier cas, elles sont composées de panneaux de taille identique qui s'accrochent les uns aux autres pour donner naissance à un meuble fonctionnel. Ce meuble peut, de surcroît, être prolongé lorsque c'est nécessaire et s'adapter à tout espace particulier.

MODULREGALE KÖNNEN massgefertigt sein, oder vorgefertigt, um sie im Haus zusammenzubauen. Letztere bestehen aus identischen Platten, die zusammengefügt werden bis sie ein funktionelles Möbel bilden. Ausserdem bieten sie, wenn die Notwendigkeit besteht, die Möglichkeit weitere Teile zu ergänzen und sich an die speziellen Gegebenheiten im Raum anzupassen.

IN A DOUBLE HEIGHT ROOM, it is a good idea to extend the library along two levels using the same panel style on both parts in order to generate a feeling of continuity. Volumes can be protected by using sets of books so their weight helps provide stability and solidity, as well as affording a touch of sophistication to the space.

SI SE CUENTA CON DOBLE ALTURA, una buena solución es prolongar la biblioteca en los dos niveles conservando el mismo estilo de paneles en ambas partes para no perder la sensación de continuidad. Con el fin de proteger los volúmenes, se puede emplear grupos de libros para que hagan peso y esto ayude a su estabilidad y sujeción, que además brinden un toque de sofisticación al espacio.

DANS UNE PIÈCE À DOUBLE HAUTEUR DE PLAFOND, le mieux est d'aménager une bibliothèque qui couvre toute la hauteur du mur avec un style uniforme pour ne pas nuire à la sensation de continuité. Pour des raisons de sécurité, on conseillera alors de placer régulièrement des livres par groupes pour des questions de poids et d'équilibre. Au point de vue décoratif, c'est en plus faire preuve d'une certaine originalité.

WENN SIE ÜBER ZWEI ETAGEN GEHT, ist es eine gute Lösung die Bibliothek über beide auszuweiten, den Stil der Regale in beiden Etagen bewahrend, um nicht den Eindruck von Kontinuität zu verlieren. Man kann, um die Bände zu schützen, die Bücher in Gruppen anordnen, damit sie sich durch ihr Gewicht Stabilität und Halt geben, was dem Raum ausserdem einen raffinierten Hauch gibt.

It is recommendable to bear in mind that any items placed on the shelves, including book covers, are a part of the décor and infuse the area with style.

Hay que tener presente que los elementos que se colocan sobre las repisas, incluyendo los forros de los propios libros, forman parte integral de la decoración y aportan estilo al área.

Il ne faut jamais oublier que les volumes placés sur les étagères, y compris les reliures des livres, jouent un rôle à part entière dans la décoration de la pièce et définissent un style particulier.

Man sollte immer daran denken, dass alles was man in den Regalen aufstellt, einschliesslich der Umschläge der Bücher selbst, Teil der Dekoration ist und zum Stil des Raumes beiträgt.

kitchens and dining rooms
cocinas y comedores
cuisines et salles à manger
küchen und esszimmer

cupboards
alacenas
placards
vorratsschränke

KITCHENS require a host of places for keeping things ranging from dried, canned, packeted and bottled foodstuffs to food that needs to be kept in refrigeration, passing through an array of utensils, pots, pans and cutlery, along with other things for cooking or eating. Most perishable goods and foodstuffs are kept on cupboard shelves, thereby affording the latter primary status.

LA COCINA demanda un cúmulo de sitios para guardar desde alimentos secos, en lata, empaquetados y embotellados, hasta aquellos que requieren refrigeración, pasando por una gran cantidad de utensilios, ollas, sartenes, cubiertos, entre otros artículos necesarios para cocinar o comer. La mayor parte de los perecederos y enseres se resguardan en las estanterías de las alacenas, por lo que éstas se convierten en muebles fundamentales.

LA CUISINE exige un grand nombre d'endroits pour y ranger des denrées (en conserve, en paquet, en boite, en bouteille et au frigo) et du matériel (ustensiles, casseroles, poêles, couverts, pour ne mentionner que quelques articles nécessaires pour cuisiner et manger). La majeure partie de ces produits périssables et du matériel trouve sa place sur les étagères des placards qui sont donc des meubles essentiels dans une cuisine.

KÜCHEN erfordern viel Platz zur Aufbewahrung, von getrockneten Lebensmitteln, Dosen, Paketen und Flaschen bis zu jenen, die gekühlt werden müssen, einer grossen Anzahl von Küchenutensilien, Töpfen, Pfannen, Besteck und anderen Dingen, die zum Kochen oder Essen notwendig sind. Der grösste Teil der haltbaren Lebensmittel wird in den Küchenschränken aufbewahrt, wodurch sie sich in fundamentale Möbel verwandeln.

CONTEMPORARY CUPBOARDS are made with simple shapes and right angles. They are comprised by modules that are joined together in adaptation to each specific area. While their functional undertaking is vital, the way they look is also important, which means the finishes of their surfaces need to be perfect. Laminated plastic is a tough, easy-to-clean material that looks great.

LAS ALACENAS CONTEMPORÁNEAS poseen formas simples y ángulos rectos. Se conforman de módulos que se van uniendo unos con otros adaptándose a cada área. Si bien su rol funcional es medular, no deja de ser relevante su estética. Por ello, los acabados de las cubiertas se vuelven protagónicos. El plástico laminado es un material resistente, fácil de limpiar y muy lucidor.

LES PLACARDS ACTUELS sont de formes simples avec des angles droits. On les aménage en unissant des modules les uns aux autres en fonction des caractéristiques de l'espace disponible. Si un placard doit avant tout être fonctionnel, son esthétique ne doit pas être ignorée pour autant. Les finitions du revêtement sont ainsi essentielles. Le plastique laminé, par exemple, est à la fois très esthétique, résistant et facile à entretenir.

MODERNE KÜCHENSCHRÄNKE sind von schlichter Form und rechten Winkeln. Sie bestehen aus Modulen, die zusammengesetzt werden und sich an jeglichen Bereich anpassen lassen. Auch wenn ihre funktionelle Rolle wesentlich ist, ist ihre ästhetische Bedeutung nicht zu vernachlässigen. Daher wird die Verarbeitung der Oberflächen zur Hauptsache. Plastikbeschichtungen sind widerstandsfähig, einfach zu reinigen und sehen sehr gut aus.

HANDLES, IRONWORKS, RAILS OR GUIDES AND DAMPING SYSTEMS allow different objects to be fully extended or slide along to provide access to food and cooking utensils. The useful life of the piece of furniture in question will depend on the quality of these mechanisms. Some ironworks are positioned so they can be seen and their design affords them a significant decorative role.

LAS JALADERAS, HERRAJES, RIELES O SISTEMAS DE GUÍAS y amortiguación son implementos que permiten la extensión total y el deslizamiento de las diferentes piezas facilitando el acceso a los alimentos y utensilios; de su buena calidad depende la vida útil del mueble. Hay herrajes que quedan a la vista, con diseños que los vuelven complementos decorativos importantes.

LES POIGNÉES, FERRURES, RAINURES, AMORTISSEURS et autres systèmes à glissières permettent d'ouvrir un tiroir, un placard dans sa totalité afin d'avoir facilement accès aux aliments ou au matériel. Une bonne qualité est primordiale pour que ces objets aient une longue durée de vie. Certaines ferrures restent visibles à l'œil nu car leur design joue un rôle important dans la décoration.

GRIFFE, BESCHLÄGE, SCHIENEN UND SCHUBLADENSYSTEME sind Hilfen, die das vollständig Ausziehen und leichte Schieben der einzelnden Elemente erleichtern und damit den Zugriff auf die Lebensmittel und Utensilien erleichtern; von ihrer Qualität hängt die Lebensdauer des Möbels ab. Es gibt Beschläge, die sichtbar bleiben, mit einem Design, das sie zu einem wichtigen Bestandteil der Dekoration macht.

EVEN IF THE TERM CUPBOARD encompasses different types of storage spaces in the kitchen, they are categorized in terms of their location into high, low, cabinets and drawers. A shallow shelf panel can store things you need to keep handy. A combination of dark and pale woods makes a superb decorative contribution.

AUN CUANDO EL TÉRMINO ALACENA abarca todos los estantes de guardado de la cocina, éstos se distinguen según su ubicación en superiores, inferiores, armarios y cajoneras. Las puertas pueden ser corredizas o abatibles. Los entrepaños poco profundos sirven para almacenar las cosas que se requiere que estén muy accesibles. Una combinación de maderas claras y oscuras ayudan a acrecentar el sentido decorativo.

BIEN QUE LE TERME DE PLACARD fasse référence à tous les types de mobilier à étagères dans une cuisine, l'emplacement de ce meuble apporte plus de détails (inférieur, supérieur, garde-manger, commode). Leurs portes peuvent coulisser ou se rabattre, leurs compartiments sont parfois peu profonds pour facilement atteindre ce que l'on y cherche, etc. Et le fait d'associer des bois clairs avec d'autres plus foncés renforcera les effets de la décoration.

AUCH WENN DER BEGRIFF Vorratsschrank alle Schränke der Küche einschliesst, unterscheiden sie sich doch durch ihre Lage in Hänge- und Unterschränke, Schränke und Schubladenschränke. Die Türen können Schiebetüren oder Klapptüren sein. Nicht sehr tiefe Regale kann man zur Unterbringung von Dingen verwenden, die schnell erreichbar sein müssen. Eine Kombination von dunklem und hellem Holz hilft den dekorativen Effekt zu vergrössern.

IF THE SPACE IS NARROW, then you need to make the most of every little nook and cranny by installing floor to ceiling cupboards all along the walls. A finish in a lively tone will help infuse the area with character, although care must be taken to make sure the colors of the wall, floor, ceiling and cupboards are well balanced.

SI EL ESPACIO ES ESTRECHO hay que intentar sacar ventaja hasta del último rincón, instalando alacenas de piso a techo y a todo lo largo de los muros. Optar por un revestimiento en un tono enérgico coopera a darle carácter a la zona, aunque hay que cuidar que los colores de la pared, del piso, del techo y de los gabinetes queden balanceados.

LORSQUE LA PIÈCE EST ÉTROITE, il faut essayer de profiter au maximum de chaque recoin avec des étagères qui vont du sol au plafond et sur toute la largeur des murs. Si l'on choisit un revêtement de teinte vive, l'endroit n'en apparaîtra que plus dynamique. Il faut cependant veiller à conserver un certain équilibre entre les couleurs du mur, du sol et des placards.

WENN DER PLATZ beschränkt ist, sollte man versuchen auch den letzten Winktel zu nutzen, in dem man Schränke vom Boden bis zur Decke und über die gesamte Länge der Wände, anbaut. Eine leuchtende Farbe für die Beschichtung zu wählen gibt dem Bereich Charakter, obwohl man darauf achten sollte, dass die Farben der Wände, des Bodens, der Decke und der Schränke im Gleichgewicht stehen.

THE TWO PREPARATION AREAS – hot and cold – should be separated from each other, while the most commonly used kitchen utensils should be on hand. Certain types of corner furniture feature rotating organizers that serve both areas, storing things like vinegar, oil, honey, sugar and condiments, to mention but a few of the numerous ingredients used every day for cooking.

CONVIENE QUE LAS DOS ÁREAS DE PREPARACIÓN –caliente y fría– estén separadas una de la otra; y que los utensilios que más se empleen en cada una se encuentren a la mano. Algunos muebles esquineros poseen organizadores rotatorios que sirven a las dos zonas, para colocar vinagre, aceite, mieles, azúcar y condimentos, entre una lista de ingredientes usados en la cocina de manera cotidiana.

BIEN SÉPARER LES DEUX PLANS DE TRAVAIL (froid, chaud) est recommandé. Il est également nécessaire que le matériel souvent utilisé dans ces deux endroits reste à portée de main. Quant aux meubles en coin, certains sont dotés d'un plateau tournant pour avoir accès au vinaigre, huile, miel, sucre et condiments, pour ne citer que quelques ingrédients utilisés tous les jours dans une cuisine.

DIE BEIDEN ARBEITSBEREICHE – heiss und kalt – sollten von einander getrennt sein; und die Utensilien, die jeweils in den Bereichen am meisten benutzt werden, sollten zur Hand sein. Einige Eckmöbel mit drehbaren Fächern können für beide Bereiche benutzt werden, um Essig, Öl, Honig, Zucker, Gewürze und andere Zutaten, die tägliche in der Küche verwendet werden, unterzubringen.

preparation areas
áreas de preparación
plans de travail
arbeitsbereiche

A SINGLE ISLE, if it is long enough, can cover the humid, cold and hot areas. In this case, the humid area should be next to the cold preparation area and then the hot area. This sequence reflects how food is actually prepared. The lower drawers in the isles are deep and can be designed long.

SI TIENE UN LARGO SUFICIENTE, una sola isla puede integrar las áreas húmeda, fría y caliente. Si es el caso, es importante que la húmeda se encuentre contigua a la de preparado en frío y la caliente enseguida. Este orden corresponde al sentido real en el que se realiza la preparación. Las cajoneras inferiores de las islas tienen buena profundidad y pueden diseñarse muy largas.

LORSQUE LA LONGUEUR de la cuisine est assez importante, un seul îlot est parfois suffisant pour y regrouper les zones humide, froide et chaude. Dans ces cas-ci, la zone humide doit être accolée à celle des préparations froides, qui, à son tour, donnera sur celle des plats chauds. Cet ordre correspond à celui qui régit le travail de cuisine. Quant aux tiroirs dans le bas de l'îlot, ils doivent être de profondeur et de longueur importantes.

WENN SIE LANG genug ist, kann eine einzige Insel die Nass-, Kalt- und Heissbereiche enthalten. Wenn das so ist, ist es wichtig, dass die Nasszone sich an den Bereich der kalten Zubereitung anschliesst und der Heissbereich folgt. Diese Reihenfolge entspricht der, in der die Speisen zubereitet werden. Die Schubladen im unteren Teil der Insel sind sehr tief und können sehr lang entworfen werden.

The size of an isle depends on the space available. If there is furniture at the front, it is a good idea to make sure there is enough room to open cupboard doors and drawers.

La dimensión de una isla depende de la espacialidad. Cuando tienen muebles en frente, es necesario asegurarse de que exista el área suficiente para abrir las puertas de las alacenas y los cajones.

Les dimensions d'un îlot dépendent des caractéristiques de la cuisine. Lorsque des meubles lui font face, il faut s'assurer qu'il y a suffisamment d'espace pour pouvoir ouvrir les portes et les tiroirs des placards.

Die Ausmasse einer Insel hängen von den räumlichen Begebenheiten ab. Wenn es ihr gegenüber Möbel gibt, sollte man sicherstellen, dass der Platz ausreicht, um die Schranktüren und Schubladen zu öffnen.

A HIGHLY PRACTICAL DESIGN SOLUTION involves installing the hot zone on an isle with the cupboards fixed to the wall. Beneath the hotplate there must be enough space to store pots, pans and other utensils needed to get the job done. The isle can also serve as a bar area adjoining the dining room if a few tall stools are included.

UNA SOLUCIÓN DE DISEÑO MUY FUNCIONAL consiste en instalar la zona caliente en una isla y las alacenas adosadas a los muros. En la parte inferior de la placa de cocción debe haber espacio suficiente para guardar ollas, sartenes y los utensilios necesarios para facilitar el trabajo. La isla puede servir también de zona de barra de antecomedor si se le complementa con algunos bancos altos.

SITUER LA ZONE CHAUDE SUR UN ÎLOT et les placards contre les murs est une solution décorative très fonctionnelle. L'espace sous les plaques de cuisson doit être assez ample pour pouvoir y mettre des casseroles, des poêles et autres ustensiles qui facilitent le travail. L'îlot peut également s'utiliser comme comptoir pour créer un coin repas si on lui ajoute quelques tabourets de haute taille.

EINE SEHR FUNKTIONELLE DESIGNLÖSUNG ist es, die Heisszone in einer Insel zu installieren und die Schränke an die Wände anzubauen. Unter der Kochfläche sollte ausreichend Platz sein um Töpfe, Pfannen und die notwendigen Utensilien unterzubringen, um die Arbeit zu erleichtern. Die Insel kann auch auch als Anrichte benutzt werden, wenn sie mit ein paar hohen Hockern komplettiert wird.

If the cupboard doors in the preparation area do not have handles, then they should have some kind of pressure mechanism to allow the doors to be opened and closed quickly.

Si las alacenas de las puertas del área de preparado no tienen jaladeras, es importante que cuenten con un mecanismo a presión que permita abrir y cerrarlas con rapidez.

Lorsque les portes des placards ne sont pas équipées de poignée dans la zone de travail, il est important de les munir avec un mécanisme à pression pour les ouvrir et les fermer rapidement.

Wenn die Türen der Schränke im Bereich der Zubereitung keine Griffe haben, sollten sie über einen Druckmechanismus verfügen, der ein schnelles Öffnen und Schliessen erlaubt.

THE ARRANGEMENT OF CUPBOARDS IN AN "L" shape helps cooking because it brings the different areas closer together. Throwing in a bar is an excellent way to increase space in the cold preparation area and can also be where meals are eaten with the help of a few stools. The surfaces of these items of furniture should be smooth and polished, because they will be easier to clean.

LA DISTRIBUCIÓN DE LAS ALACENAS EN "L" facilita el cocinado, pues acorta la distancia entre una zona y otra. Incluir una barra es un excelente recurso para ampliar el espacio de preparación en frío y a la vez puede servir para comer si se le añaden unos bancos. Es preferible que las cubiertas de estos muebles sean lisas y pulidas, pues ello simplifica su limpieza.

UNE DISTRIBUTION DES PLACARDS EN FORME DE "L" facilite le travail de la cuisine car les distances entre les zones sont réduites. Le fait d'aménager un comptoir est un bon moyen d'agrandir l'espace des préparations froides et on peut aussi utiliser cet endroit pour s'y restaurer si on le complète avec quelques tabourets. Quant au revêtement de tous ces meubles, il vaut mieux qu'il soit lisse et bien poli afin de facilement les maintenir propres.

DIE ANORDNUNG DER SCHRÄNKE IN "L" Form erleichtert das Kochen, da es die Entfernung zwischen den Bereichen verkürzt. Eine Theke einzubauen, ist ausgezeichnet, um den Platz im Bereich der Zubereitung zu vergrössern und sie kann gleichzeitig zum Essen benutzt werden, wenn einige Hocker ergänzt werden. Die Oberflächen der Möbel sollten glatt und glänzend sein, da es die Reinigung erleichtert.

A MULTIFUNCTIONAL ISLE that resolves needs regarding cleaning, and cold and hot preparation, and includes shelves for storing things and even for eating on is ideal for smaller spaces. In this option, the sink needs to be double size or very big in order to provide space for dishes to drain off. The other items of furniture can be fixed to a nearby wall.

UNA ISLA MULTIFUNCIONAL que resuelva las necesidades de limpieza, preparación en frío y caliente, incluya anaqueles para guardado y hasta barra para comer, funciona de maravilla para espacios pequeños. En esta alternativa es sustancial que la tarja sea doble o muy grande para tener sitio donde escurrir los trastes. El resto de los enseres pueden quedar empotrados en un muro aledaño.

UN ÎLOT MULTIFONCTIONNEL où l'on peut procéder aux travaux d'hygiène, aux préparations froides et chaudes, avec des étagères et un comptoir pour manger, fonctionne à merveille dans une petite cuisine. Dans ce cas, l'évier doit être double ou très grand afin d'y faire sécher la vaisselle. Le reste du matériel de cuisine, peut, lui, rester dans des meubles encastrés sur un mur proche.

EINE MULTIFUNKTIONELLE INSEL, die die Notwendigkeiten der Säuberung, kalter und warmer Zubereitung löst, Staumöglichkeiten bietet und sogar eine Theke zum Essen beinhaltet, ist eine wundervolle Lösung für kleine Räume. Bei dieser Möglichkeit ist es unabdinglich, dass es doppelte Spülbecken oder zumindest ein sehr grosses gibt, um einen Platz zum Abwaschen zu haben. Die restlichen Einrichtungsgegenstände können in angrenzende Wände eingebaut werden.

carving units
trinchadores
buffets
anrichten

CARVING UNITS are items of furniture that complement the dining room and increase storage space. If they are made in the same style and with the same colors as the rest of the furniture, they will blend in perfectly. They are commonly used for storing napkins, tablecloths, glassware, plates and cutlery, as well as other articles such as candle holders, candles, under plates and other ornamental objects that go on the table.

LOS TRINCHADORES son muebles que complementan el comedor, a través de los cuales se extiende el espacio de guardado. Si mantienen el estilo y colorido del resto del mobiliario, lucen totalmente armónicos. Por lo general dentro de ellos se almacena la mantelería, cristalería, vajillas y cubiertos. También sirven para resguardar candelabros, velas, bajo platos y otros elementos de ornato que se colocan en la mesa.

LES BUFFETS sont des meubles qui complètent ceux présents dans une salle à manger et qui ont pour fonction d'améliorer les capacités de rangement de cette pièce. Si leur style et leur couleur ne diffèrent pas du reste de la pièce, l'harmonie règnera totalement. Dans les buffets, on conserve en général le linge de table, la verrerie, la vaisselle et les couverts. On peut également y placer des chandeliers, des bougies, des dessous-de-plat et autres accessoires qui embellissent la table.

ANRICHTEN sind Möbel, die das Esszimmer vervollständigen und den Stauraum vergrössern. Wenn sie den Stil und die Farbe der restlichen Möbel bewahren, fügen sie sich harmonisch ein. Normalerweise werden in ihnen Tischdecken, Gläser, Geschirr und Besteck aufbewahrt. Sie können auch dazu dienen Kerzenständer, Kerzen, Platzteller und andere Tischdekoration unterzubringen.

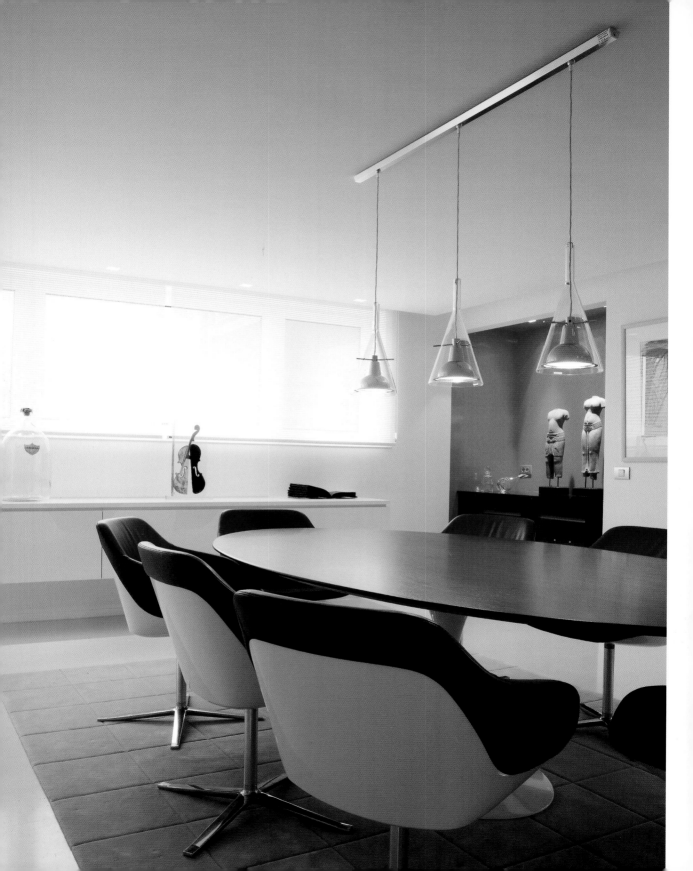

These items of furniture are also called buffets, and they look great if they are custom designed and embedded in the wall. If they are raised, they look spectacular thanks to their toned visual impact.

Estos muebles, también llamados buffets, se destacan cuando su diseño es a medida y se les empotra en la pared. Se ven particularmente estéticos si son volados, pues su peso visual se aligera.

L'esthétique des buffets est particulièrement évidente lorsqu'ils sont fabriqués sur mesure et adossés à un mur. S'ils ne reposent pas sur le sol, leur beauté n'en sera que plus indéniable encore car ils paraîtront plus légers.

Diese Möbel, auch Buffets genannt, stechen heraus, wenn sie nach Mass entworfen wurden und in die Wand eingebaut sind. Besonders ästhetisch sehen sie aus, wenn sie frei hängen, da ihr optisches Gewicht verringert wird.

A CONSOLE TABLE can take the place of the buffet in the dining room, even though it does not offer any storage space, because it is useful for the practical side of the service. When it is not being used, its contribution will be decorative. Its beauty can be emphasized with a vase, which will highlight its symmetry when placed in the middle, while setting it to one side will create an impression of great vitality.

UNA CONSOLA puede sustituir al buffet del comedor, aunque no cuente con espacio de guardado, pues se usa para la parte práctica del servicio. Mientras no se use, su función se puede reducir meramente al aspecto decorativo. Su belleza se realza con un florero, que si se pone al centro exalta la simetría y si se recarga a uno de los lados da la impresión de mayor dinamismo.

UNE CONSOLE peut remplacer un buffet dans la salle à manger. Ce n'est pas un meuble de rangement puisqu'on l'utilise tous les jours. Fermé, sa fonction est principalement décorative et sa beauté n'en ressort que mieux avec un vase à fleur posé dessus. Lorsque ce dernier est placé exactement au centre, la symétrie du meuble est mise en valeur. Mais situé sur un des côtés du placard, le vase dynamisera la pièce.

EINE KONSOLE kann ein Buffet im Esszimmer ersetzen, obwohl sie nicht über Stauraum verfügt, da sie für den praktischen Teil des Servierens benutzt wird. Während sie nicht genutzt wird, beschränkt sich ihre Funktion auf einen rein dekorativen Aspekt. Ihre Schönheit kann man mit einer Blumenvase betonen, die, wenn sie in der Mitte steht, die Symmetrie unterstreicht und, wenn sie auf einer der beiden Seiten steht, Dynamik verleiht.

FROM A DECORATIVE POINT OF VIEW, the carving unit can become a focal point in the dining room if its design is potent enough. One good way of bolstering its presence and character is by hanging adornments or works of art on the wall where it is located. The mix of tones and materials in a single item of furniture also boosts its visual appeal.

DESDE LA PERSPECTIVA DEL DECORADO, el trinchador consigue convertirse en el elemento focal de la habitación si sobresale por su diseño. Para reforzar su presencia y carácter es recomendable colgar adornos o piezas de arte en el muro donde se encuentre. La mezcla de tonos y materiales en un solo mueble coopera también a aumentar su atractivo.

AU POINT DE VUE DÉCORATIF, un buffet devient l'élément-clé de la pièce si son design est bien travaillé. Pour en souligner la présence et les caractéristiques, il est conseillé de placer des accessoires et des objets d'art sur le mur contre lequel il repose. Plusieurs teintes et matériaux pour un seul meuble contribuent également à sa mise en valeur.

AUS DER SICHT DER DEKORATION kann eine Anrichte sich in den Blickfang des Raumes verwandeln, wenn sie durch ihr Design hervorsticht. Um ihre Präsenz und ihren Charakter zu verstärken, sollten Dekorationsstücke an der Wand, an der sie steht, angebracht werden. Die Mischung aus Farbtönen und Materialien in einem einzigen Möbelstück, trägt auch dazu bei, seine Attraktivität zu erhöhen.

Woods that display their veining are ideal for bringing out the full
beauty of a buffet and making it a fundamental part of the area's
decoration.

Las maderas que evidencian su veteado son perfectas para hacer
descollar la belleza de un buffet, volviéndose parte fundamental
del decorado del área.

Les veines naturelles apparentes de certains bois sont parfaites pour
souligner la beauté d'un buffet qui joue alors un rôle clé dans la
décoration de la pièce.

Holzarten, deren Maserung deutlich zu sehen ist, sind perfekt um die
Schönheit eines Buffets zu betonen, es in den wesentlichen Teil der
Dekoration dieses Bereiches verwandelnd.

bedrooms & bathrooms
recámaras y baños
chambres et salles de bain
schlafzimmer und badezimmer

bureaus and drawers
burós y cajoneras
tables de nuit et commodes
nachtschränke und kommoden

BUREAUS AND DRAWERS MIGHT BE SIMPLE, but they are extremely useful in the bedroom. If they are long and deep then they are even more welcome. It is important to know exactly what is going to be put inside them in order to decide how tall they need to be. The ones that are opened and closed with sliding mechanisms and have a channel on the inside for the fingers are very practical indeed.

POR SIMPLES QUE SEAN, LOS BURÓS Y LAS CAJONERAS son elementos de gran utilidad en las recámaras. Cuando son largos y profundos son muy aprovechables. Es fundamental saber qué se va a colocar en ellos para planear su altura. Los que tienen sistemas deslizables para abrir y cerrar, con canal interior para manipularlos con los dedos son muy cómodos.

D'APPARENCE SIMPLE, LES TABLES DE NUIT ET LES COMMODES sont des éléments très utiles dans une chambre. Pour bien en profiter, il vaut mieux qu'elles soient larges et profondes. Mais il faut d'abord savoir ce que l'on va y mettre pour en prévoir la hauteur. Celles qui comportent des tiroirs coulissants, avec des systèmes à glissières pour les ouvrir à la main, sont très pratiques.

NACHTTISCHE UND KOMMODEN mögen einfache Möbel sein, aber sie sind im Schlafzimmer extrem praktisch. Wenn sie lang und tief sind sie noch mehr willkommen. Es ist von wesentlicher Bedeutung zu wissen, was man in ihnen unterbringen möchte, um ihre Höhe zu planen. Weisen sie ein Schiebesystem zum Öffnen und Schliessen auf, mit einem inneren Kanal, der mit den Fingern bedient wird, sind sie sehr bequem.

BUREAUS WITHOUT DRAWERS are like support tables and can look really good thanks to their lightness. This type of furniture can be integrated into two panels and create a modular item that doubles up as a headboard to increase storage space in the bedroom. Shelves offer surfaces for books, photos, decorations and other favorites.

LOS BURÓS SIN CAJONERAS funcionan como mesas de apoyo, por su liviandad se convierten en piezas altamente estéticas. Para ganar espacio de guardado en la habitación, este tipo de muebles puede integrarse a dos entrepaños y conformar un modular que haga las veces de cabecera. Las repisas se convierten en auxiliares para almacenar libros, fotografías, adornos y cosas preferidas.

LES TABLES DE NUIT SANS TIROIR peuvent être utilisées comme tables d'appoint. Parce que leur apparence reste sobre, ce sont des meubles très esthétiques. Pour accroître les capacités de rangement de la chambre, ce type de meuble peut trouver sa place contre une cloison et prolonger la tête de lit. Et les tablettes deviennent des endroits pour y poser des livres, des photos, des accessoires décoratifs ou des objets de prédilection.

NACHTTISCHE OHNE SCHUBLADEN dienen als zusätzliche Tische, durch ihre Leichtigkeit werden sie zu hoch ästhetischen Stücken. Um Stauraum zu gewinnen kann man diese Möbel zwischen zwei Platten in ein Modul integrieren, das gleichzeitig als Kopfstück des Bettes dient. Die Regalbretter helfen Bücher, Fotos, Dekorationsgegenstände und persönliche Objekte unterzubringen.

DRESSERS TODAY ARE DESIGNED with pure lines and right angles, and boast both appearance and practicality. Most of them have large drawers that help keep order in the bedroom. If they have compartments, they can even be used to store first aid articles, sewing implements, underwear, shawls, handkerchiefs, stockings, cosmetics, and a whole host of other objects. The surface tends to be purely decorative.

EN LA ACTUALIDAD LAS CÓMODAS SON DISEÑADAS a partir de líneas puras y ángulos rectos, combinando estética y funcionalidad. La mayor parte de ellas posee grandes cajones que ayudan a mantener un orden en la habitación, cuando éstos tienen compartimientos sirven hasta para guardar artículos de botiquín, costureros, ropa interior, pañoletas, pañuelos, medias, cosméticos, entre una serie de objetos. Por lo general, su cubierta es meramente decorativa.

LE DESIGN ACTUEL DES COMMODES, qui associe fonctionnalité et esthétique, est à base de lignes pures et d'angles droits. La majeure partie d'entre elles sont dotées de grands tiroirs pour maintenir l'ordre dans la chambre. Lorsque ces derniers sont divisés en plusieurs espaces, on peut y déposer, entre autres, une trousse à pharmacie, une boîte à couture, des sous-vêtements, des foulards, des mouchoirs, des bas, des produits de beauté. Et les dessus de commode sont en général très esthétiques.

Heutzutage werden Kommoden von reinen Linien und rechten Winkeln ausgehend entworfen, Ästhetik mit Funktionalität verbindend. Die meisten haben grosse Schubladen, die dabei helfen, Ordnung im Raum zu halten und wenn diese Fächer haben, können sie dazu dienen Medikamente, Nähzeug, Unterwäsche, Tücher, Taschentücher, Strumpfhosen, Kosmetika und vieles mehr, unterzubringen. Normalerweise ist ihre Beschichtung hochdekorativ.

INCLUDING A VINTAGE DRESSER in a modern bedroom will provide a touch of stylishness and create a delightful contrast with the rest of the furniture. Some dressers designed back in the 1940s are exquisitely proportioned, as are their drawers, while their shapes are simple and bring out the full splendor of the wood.

INCLUIR UNA CÓMODA VINTAGE en una recámara moderna le da un toque de elegancia al área y genera un contraste fascinante con el resto del mobiliario. Algunas de estos muebles que fueron diseñados durante los cuarenta del siglo pasado contaban con proporciones exquisitas tanto en el mueble en sí como en sus cajones, sus formas eran simples y exaltaban el lucimiento de la madera.

PLACER UNE COMMODE D'ÉPOQUE dans une chambre moderne donne à la pièce un air raffiné et génère un contraste fascinant au niveau du mobilier. Les proportions de certaines de ces créations d'époque, qui ont été fabriquées dans les années 40 du XXe siècle, étaient très bien équilibrées tant au niveau du meuble lui-même que de ses tiroirs. Et leurs formes simples mettaient en valeur la beauté du bois.

EINE KOMMODE IM VINTAGE Stil in einem modernen Schlafzimmer aufzustellen, gibt dem Raum einen Hauch Eleganz und steht in einem faszinierenden Kontrast zu den restlichen Möbeln. Einige dieser, in den vierziger Jahren des letzten Jahrhunderts entworfenen Möbel, sind von exquisiter Proportion, sowohl das Möbelstück selbst, als auch in seinen Schubladen, seine Form ist schlicht und betont die Schönheit des Holzes.

dressing rooms
vestidores
dressings
ankleidezimmer

ONE THING THAT DEFINITELY NEEDS a suitable place for storage is clothing. Garments for different seasons of the year are a universe in themselves, especially if we consider the range of accessories, shoes, bags, jewelry, handkerchiefs and whites, each of which should ideally have a place assigned just for them. An orderly dressing room isn't just useful; it can become a joy to be in if its style is kept simple.

ENTRE LAS COSAS QUE MÁS REQUIEREN de un sitio adecuado para guardado está la ropa. La vestimenta para las diferentes estaciones del año es todo un tema, así como la variedad de accesorios, zapatos, bolsas, joyas, pañuelos y a veces los blancos, que idealmente deben tener un lugar asignado. Un vestidor ordenado no sólo es útil, sino que se convierte en un cuarto agradable si su estilo es depurado.

LES VÊTEMENTS SONT LES OBJETS QUI NÉCESSITENT le plus une pièce particulière. Ils ont besoin d'être rangés par saison tout comme les accessoires, les chaussures, les sacs, les bijoux, les mouchoirs et parfois même la literie qui doivent être conservés dans un endroit qui leur est propre. Un dressing bien organisé n'est pas seulement utile. C'est également une pièce agréable si son style est épuré.

UNTER DEN DINGEN, die am meisten einen angemessenen Stauraum brauchen, ist die Kleidung. Die Kleidung für die verschiedenen Jahreszeiten ist immer ein Thema, so wie auch die Vielzahl des Zubehörs, Schuhe, Taschen, Schmuck, Tücher und manchmal auch Bettwäsche, die im Idealfall einen eigenen Bereich haben sollte. Ein ordentlicher Ankleideraum ist nicht nur nützlich, sondern wird zu einem angenehmen Raum, wenn sein Stil rein ist.

The choice of whether or not to put doors on the dressing room depends on individual preference, but one benefit they certainly provide is that they will protect clothing from dust.

La alternativa de colocar puertas o no en el vestidor depende de las preferencias personales, entre las ventajas que éstas ofrecen está el resguardar la ropa del polvo.

Équiper un dressing de portes ou non dépend des goûts de chacun. Avec, les vêtements pourront être conservés à l'abri de la poussière.

Die Frage, ob man im Ankleideraum Türen anbringt, hängt von den Vorzügen jedes einzelnen ab, ein Vorteil besteht darin, dass sie die Kleidung vor Staub schützen.

DOORLESS DRESSING ROOMS with bare hangers are very practical for selecting clothes, because everything is on view. A few shelf panels for folded items of clothing are always a good bet. It is advisable to have some drawers for smaller items of clothing and accessories. Decorated boxes fit in with the overall look and are used for keeping things that are not used every day.

LOS VESTIDORES SIN PUERTAS, con los colgadores aparentes, son muy prácticos para seleccionar la ropa, pues todo queda a la vista. Colocar algunos entrepaños para la ropa doblada es una buena opción. Para la ropa pequeña y los accesorios es preferible que haya algunas cajoneras. Las cajas decoradas se usan para guardar cosas que no son de uso diario y no desentonan con el aspecto estético.

LES DRESSINGS SANS PORTE, avec les vêtements apparents, sont très pratiques pour faire son choix parce que tout reste visible. Quelques étagères pour les vêtements pliés est une bonne idée. Pour les vêtements de petite taille et les accessoires, il est préférable de prévoir des tiroirs. Quant aux coffres décorés dont l'apparence ne jure pas avec le style général, on les utilise pour y ranger des choses que l'on emploie rarement.

ANKLEIDERÄUME OHNE TÜREN, mit den Kleiderstangen sichtbar, sind sehr praktisch, um die Kleidung zu wählen, da alles sichtbar ist. Einige Regalbretter für gefaltete Wäsche anzubringen ist eine gute Option. Für kleine Kleidungsstücke und dem Zubehör sind einige Schubladen zu empfehlen. Dekorative Schachteln eignen sich um Dinge aufzubewahren, die nicht täglich benutzt werden und stören den ästhetischen Eindruck nicht.

A COMBINATION OF STORAGE FURNITURE in a shared dressing room is ideal, especially if the design considers storage measurements for things like shoes, handbags, accessories or jewelry, among many others. If the collection of jewels and accessories is substantial, a central isle with a window and drawers is very practical. A set of stools is another great option for the area in the middle.

LA MEZCLA DE ELEMENTOS DE GUARDADO en un vestidor compartido es idónea, sobre todo si el diseño contempla las medidas de almacenaje de artículos como zapatos, bolsos de mujer, accesorios o joyería, entre una larga lista. Si las joyas y accesorios son abundantes, una isla central con vitrina y cajoneras es muy funcional. Otra buena opción para la zona del centro es un juego de taburetes.

UN DRESSING DIVISÉ EN PLUSIEURS SECTIONS pour conserver une grande variété de choses est idéal, qui plus est, si le design de cette pièce a été aussi conçu pour, entre autres choses, les chaussures, les sacs féminins, les accessoires et les bijoux. Si ces deux derniers types d'objets sont en grand nombre, un îlot central doté de vitrines et de tiroirs sera très pratique. Autre solution : diviser le centre de la pièce avec plusieurs sièges.

DIE MISCHUNG AUS VERSCHIEDENEN ELEMENTEN in einem geteilten Ankleideraum ist günstig, vor allem wenn das Design die Grösse von zu lagernden Objekten wie Schuhen, Handtaschen, Zubehör, Schmuck und vielem mehr, berücksichtigt. Wenn es reichlich Schmuck und Zubehör gibt, ist eine zentrale Insel mit einer Vitrine und Schubladen sehr praktisch. Eine andere Option für den Bereich in der Mitte, ist eine Sitzgelegenheit.

bathroom furniture
muebles de baño
meubles de salle de bain
badezimmermöbel

LACK OF STORAGE SPACE is a prime consideration in the design of storage furniture for the bathroom. This is why furniture or shelves are increasingly inserted under washbasins, series of panels are fixed to the wall and complementary items are added. Even though materials and styles are highly versatile, wood and stainless steel remain the materials of choice.

LA FALTA DE ESPACIO PARA ALMACENAR es un factor determinante en el diseño de los muebles de guardado para el baño. Por esta razón, cada vez es más común incluir repisas o mobiliario debajo de los lavabos, series de entrepaños empotrados en las paredes y algunos elementos complementarios. Aun cuando los materiales y estilos son muy versátiles, el uso de la madera y el acero inoxidable sigue siendo recurrente.

UN ESPACE DE RANGEMENT restreint influence le design choisi pour les meubles de rangement dans une salle de bain. C'est en raison de cette contrainte qu'il est fréquent de placer des étagères ou des meubles sous les lavabos ou de les encastrer dans les murs ou sur un élément important dans la pièce. Même lorsque les matériaux et le style choisis sont destinés à de multiples usages, l'emploi du bois et de l'acier inoxydable reste habituel.

DER MANGEL AN STAURAUM ist ein bestimmender Faktor im Design von Badezimmermöbeln. Deshalb ist es immer üblicher Regalbretter oder Möbel unter den Waschbecken anzubringen, Serien von Regalen in die Wände einzubauen und andere ergänzende Elemente zu nutzen. Auch wenn die Materialen und Stile sehr vielfälltig sind, sind Holz und rostfreier Stahl die am meisten verwendeten.

AN EFFECTIVE WAY of creating storage space in the bathroom is with a raised item of furniture fixed to the wall under the washbasin and which makes its full length available. The fact that it is raised makes it look lighter and helps cleaning. A structure with stainless steel shelves could also serve as a towel rack.

UNA EXCELENTE MANERA de ganar capacidad de acopio en el baño es un mueble volado bajo-lavabo que quede empotrado a muro y que aproveche su longitud. El volado no sólo ofrece la sensación visual de ligereza, sino que también facilita la limpieza del sitio. No está mal prever alguna estructura auxiliar con estantes de acero inoxidable que sirva para acomodar las toallas.

UN MEUBLE ACCOLÉ SUR TOUTE la longueur d'un mur et qui ne touche pas le sol sous le lavabo constitue un excellent moyen d'accroître les possibilités de rangement d'une salle de bain. Le fait qu'il ne repose pas par terre renforce non seulement la légèreté de son apparence mais facilite également l'entretien des lieux. Et quelques accessoires supplémentaires comme des porte-serviettes en acier inoxydable ne seront pas de trop.

EINE HERVORRAGENDE Möglichkeit Stauraum im Badezimmer zu schaffen ist ein Schrank unter dem Waschbecken, in die Wand eingebaut, das seine Länge nutzt. Da es nicht bis zum Boden reicht, bietet es nicht nur den optischen Eindruck von Leichtigkeit, es erleichtert auch die Reinigung des Bereiches. Es ist nicht schlecht eine Regalstruktur aus rostfreiem Stahl einzuplanen, in dem man die Handtücher unterbringen kann.

FURNITURE UNDER THE WASHBASIN should have as many drawers or compartments as possible, as they economize space, boost storage area and allow things to be put away more quickly. The wood in these storage boxes infuses the ambience with warmth and its natural veining is instrumental in generating a suggestive and stylish atmosphere.

CONVIENE QUE EL MOBILIARIO BAJO-LAVABO cuente con el mayor número de cajones o compartimentos posibles, ya que con ello se economiza espacio, se amplía la zona para guardar y se ubican más rápido las cosas. Las maderas aparecen en estas cajas almacenadoras para dar calidez al ambiente y sus veteados naturales son la clave para generar atmósferas sugestivas y elegantes.

LE MOBILIER SOUS LE LAVABO doit comporter le plus grand nombre possible de tiroirs ou de compartiments afin d'accroître les possibilités de rangement et de gagner de l'espace et du temps lorsque l'on cherche quelque chose. Pour des meubles de rangement sous la forme de boîtes, le bois et ses veines naturelles sont tout indiqués pour réchauffer la pièce et doter celle-ci d'une atmosphère raffinée et élégante.

DIE MÖBEL UNTER DEM WASCHBECKEN SOLLTEN die grösstmögliche Anzahl Schubladen oder Fächer aufweisen, da man so Raum spart, den Stauraum erweitert und schneller Sachen findet. Holz ist bei diesen Staukästen zu finden, um dem Ambiente Wärme zu verleihen und seine natürliche Maserung ist der Schlüssel zu einer anregenden und eleganten Atmosphäre.

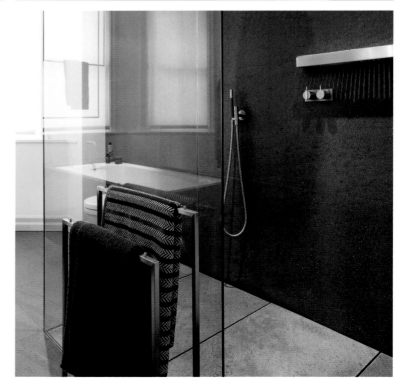

THE SYMMETRY OF STORAGE FURNITURE helps convey a sense of order, especially if the bathroom is shared. The storage surface can be extended with a couple of made-to-measure bars to hang towels from, along with a hanger for the dressing gown. A shelf in the humid area will be both comfortable and useful for putting bathroom items on.

LA SIMETRÍA DEL MUEBLE DE GUARDADO coopera a transmitir la sensación de orden, sobre todo si el baño es compartido. Para extender la superficie de almacenamiento se puede recurrir a un par de barras a medida en donde se cuelguen las toallas e incluir un gancho perchero para la bata. Asimismo, una repisa auxiliar en la zona húmeda resultará tan cómoda como útil para apoyar los artículos de aseo.

LA SYMÉTRIE D'UN MEUBLE DE RANGEMENT contribue à faire régner dans la salle de bain une certaine sensation d'ordre, surtout si cette pièce est utilisée par plusieurs personnes. Afin d'augmenter les espaces de rangements, on peut avoir recours à deux porte-serviettes faits sur mesure et à une patère pour y suspendre la robe de chambre. Une étagère d'appoint, dans la zone humide de la pièce, sera également très utile pour y poser des accessoires de toilette.

DIE SYMMETRIE DES MÖBELS hilft den Eindruck von Ordnung zu vermitteln, besonders wenn das Badezimmer geteilt wird. Um die Staufläche zu vergrössern kann man einige massgerechte Stangen für Handtücher und einen Haken für Bademäntel anbringen. Genauso ist ein Regalbrett in der Nasszone sowohl bequem, als auch nützlich um die Reinigungsmittel unterzubringen.

MODULATED AND LACQUERED FURNITURE in pure white is the best way to underscore the impression of cleanliness and harmony. If doorless shelves are used, then they should have the necessary height and depth in order to provide a truly practical solution. They are often embedded and made-to-measure, the advantage being that the things they store are handy and on view.

CUANDO SE BUSCA REFORZAR LA IMPRESIÓN de pulcritud y armonía, no hay como elegir mobiliario modulado y laqueado en color blanco puro. Si se opta por repisas sin puertas, es importante que éstas tengan la altura y profundidad necesarias para que en verdad sean funcionales. Por lo general, se trata de elementos empotrados y hechos a medida, que ofrecen la ventaja de que las cosas quedan accesibles y a la vista.

LORSQUE L'ON SOUHAITE RENFORCER LA SENSATION de propreté et d'ordre dans une salle de bain, il n'existe rien de mieux qu'un mobilier modulaire et laqué de blanc pur. Avec un meuble à étagères sans porte, il faut qu'il soit assez grand et profond pour être fonctionnel. Il s'agit, en général, de meubles faits sur mesure et encastrés pour que tout reste visible et à portée de main.

WENN MAN DEN EINDRUCK VON SAUBERKEIT und Harmonie verstärken möchte, gibt es nichts besseres als lackierte Modulmöbel in Weiss zu wählen. Wann man sich für Fächer ohne Türen entscheidet, ist es wichtig, dass diese die nötige Höhe und Tiefe haben um wirklich funtionell zu sein. Normalerweise handelt es sich um massgefertigte eingebaute Elemente, die den Vorteil haben, dass die Sachen sichtbar bleiben.

auxiliary zones
zonas auxiliares
espaces secondaires
sonstige bereiche

THERE ARE MANY WAYS to store bottles of wine and other drinks in the home. Cellars provide the perfect temperature, humidity and controlled climate conditions for storing wine. They can be made from glass and stainless steel, and designed in straight lines to look light, modern and sleek. Storage furniture can be vertical or horizontal with basic lighting providing the magic touch.

EXISTEN MÚLTIPLES OPCIONES para conservar las botellas de vino y otros bebidas en casa. Las cavas son ideales para almacenar los vinos con temperatura, humedad y clima controlados. Una alternativa es construirlas de vidrio y acero inoxidable, con un diseño de líneas rectas, que luzca ligero, contemporáneo y exquisito. El mueble puede ser vertical u horizontal y la iluminación será básica para darle el toque.

DANS UNE MAISON, on peut conserver le vin ou d'autres boissons de multiples façons. Mais les caves à vin restent idéales pour y entreposer les bouteilles à température voulue, au bon taux d'humidité et dans des conditions ad hoc. Il est possible de fabriquer ces caves avec du verre et de l'acier inoxydable, avec une forme à lignes droites pour qu'elles paraissent légères, modernes et séduisantes. Verticales ou horizontales, leur éclairage particulier les dotera d'une touche personnelle.

ES GIBT EINE VIELZAHL von Möglichkeiten, um Wein und andere Getränke im Haus zu lagern. Weinkeller sind ideal um Weine mit kontrollierter Temperatur, Feuchtigkeit und Klima zu lagern. Eine Möglichkeit besteht darin, sie aus Glas und rostfreiem Stahl zu bauen, in einem Design von geraden Linien, das leicht, zeitgenössisch und exquisit wirkt. Das Möbel kann horizontal oder vertikal sein und die Beleuchtung ist fundamental, um ihm einen besonderen Touch zu geben.

cellars and bars
cavas y bares
caves à vin et bars
weinkeller und bars

Cava

VINOS POR COPEO 5 y 10oz.

V.B. Rene Barbier Mediterranean

V.B. Diamante Semi-Dulce

Celeste Crianza

Ibéricos Crianza

Beronia Crianza

Gran Sangre de Toro

Atrium

Campo Viejo Reserva

El Vino

EVEN THOUGH THEY ARE LOCATED IN THE HOME, rooms for storing wine should have earth or gravel floors, moderate ventilation, closely controlled daylight and a temperature of between 11 and 18°C. If they are made of wood, the wood should be neutral so its fragrance doesn't contaminate the wine.

AUN CUANDO SE ENCUENTREN EN CASA, las habitaciones destinadas al almacenaje de vinos deben tener pisos húmedos de tierra o grava, ventilación moderada, luz natural muy controlada y una temperatura que oscile alrededor de los 11 y 18° C. Si están hechas de madera, es preferible que sea de alguna especie neutra, para que su olor no contamine al vino.

MÊME AU SEIN D'UNE DEMEURE, le sol des pièces destinées à la conservation du vin doit être humide et en terre ou en graviers. L'aération doit être modérée, la lumière naturelle, très contrôlée, et il est important que la température se situe constamment entre 11 et 18 degrés Celsius. Si elles sont en bois, il est préférable que celui-ci soit d'une espèce neutre pour ne pas altérer le goût du vin.

AUCH WENN SIE SICH IM HAUS befinden, müssen die Räume, die zur Weinlagerung bestimmt sind, feuchte Böden aus Erde oder Kiesel haben, eine mässige Belüftung, sehr beschränkten natürlichen Lichteinfall und eine Temperatur, die sich zwischen 11 und 18°C bewegt. Wenn die Regale aus Holz sind, sollte es eine neutrale Art sein, damit der Geruch nicht auf den Wein übergeht.

IF A CELLAR spans the full length and height of the wall and its design is simple, the lead role, visually speaking, will be awarded to the drinks it stores. It is recommendable to design cells with the right slant to keep the cork in contact with the wine, and include other shelves that are completely horizontal for holding bottles of rum, whisky, brandy, tequila and liquors, as well as other drinks.

CUANDO UNA CAVA abarca la longitud y la altura total del muro y su diseño es liviano, el rol protagónico recae en las propias bebidas que resguarda. Es conveniente pensar en celdas con un grado de inclinación para que el corcho esté en contacto con el vino e incluir otras repisas totalmente horizontales para colocar botellas de ron, whisky, brandy, tequila y licores, entre otros.

LORSQU'UNE CAVE À VIN repose sur toute la surface d'un mur et quand sa structure reste légère, ce sont les boissons entreposées qui jouent le premier rôle dans la pièce. Il est important de prévoir des clayettes légèrement inclinées pour que les bouchons restent en contact avec le vin mais d'y placer aussi des étagères, cette fois, complètement horizontales pour y poser des bouteilles de rhum, de whisky, de brandy, de téquila et autres alcools forts.

WENN EIN WEINREGAL über die gesamte Länge und Höhe einer Wand geht und sein Design leicht ist, fällt die Hauptrolle den gelagerten Getränken selbst zu. Man sollte daran denken, Fächer mit Gefälle zu planen, damit der Korken mit dem Wein in Berührung kommt und andere komplett horizontale, um Flaschen mit Rum, Whisky, Brandy, Tequila und Likören unterzubringen.

A SMALL BAR CAN BE MADE with just three narrow panels along with a contemporary style cabinet, to render the space highly decorative. The cabinet can be used to store glassware and bottles vertically, while panel shelves are ideal for keeping wine horizontal. There is no denying the sheer splendor of wooden furniture in this role.

ES FACTIBLE ARMAR UN PEQUEÑO BAR con tan solo tres entrepaños estrechos y un armario de estilo contemporáneo convirtiendo el espacio en altamente decorativo. El armario facilita el guardado de la cristalería y las botellas que se pueden apoyar de forma vertical, en tanto que los entrepaños funcionan bien para los vinos que se tienen que mantener recostados. La belleza del mobiliario de madera para estas funciones es innegable.

IL EST POSSIBLE D'AMÉNAGER UN PETIT BAR avec simplement trois étagères réduites et une armoire moderne et doter ainsi la pièce d'une certaine qualité esthétique. L'armoire facilite le rangement des verres et des bouteilles qui peuvent rester à la verticale alors que les étagères sont destinées au vin qui doit demeurer à l'horizontale. Et la beauté de ce type de mobilier, lorsqu'il est en bois, est inégalable.

ES IST MÖGLICH EINE KLEINE BAR mit nur drei langen Regalbrettern und einem zeitgenössischen Schrank herzurichten, ihn in einen hochdekorativen Bereich verwandelnd. Der Schrank erleichtert die Unterbringung von Gläsern und Flaschen, die sich liegend gegenseitig Halt geben, so dass die Fächer gut für Weine geeignet sind, die liegend gelagert werden müssen. Die Schönheit dieses Holzmöbels ist nicht zu leugnen.

Bars offer simpler alternatives to cellars. A couple of walls can be adapted with shelves so wine can be arranged in terms of type and vintage, and some drawers can be included for utensils.

Los bares son alternativas más sencillas que las cavas. Es posible adaptar uno o dos muros con estantes que permitan ordenar los vinos por tipo y fechas de cosecha e incluir algunas cajoneras para los utensilios.

Les bars sont plus faciles à installer que les caves. On place des étagères sur un ou deux murs pour classer les vins par millésimes et on y ajoute quelques tiroirs pour les ustensiles.

Bars sind einfachere Alternativen zu Weinkellern. Es ist möglich eine oder zwei Wände mit Regalen, die es erlauben die Weine nach Typ und Erntezeit zu ordnen und ein paar Schubladen für Utensilien umzubauen.

THE COMPLETE BAR, with a bar top, washbasin and storage furniture is a dream for many people thanks to the ambience of intimacy it evokes in the home. The best way to store glasses is upside-down, hanging from the base. They can also be supported with guides or flat wooden slats placed parallel to the shelves.

EL BAR COMPLETO, con barra, tarja y mobiliario de guardado es una fantasía para muchas personas. Ello se debe a que evoca un ambiente íntimo para disfrutar en casa. La manera más funcional para resguardar las copas es boca abajo, colgando de su base. Para crear un buen sostén para copas son útiles las guías o listones planos de madera, colocados en paralelo a la estantería.

UN BAR COMPLET, avec comptoir, évier et meubles de rangement est un rêve que beaucoup de gens caressent. Cet attrait est probablement dû à cette atmosphère intime que l'on peut recréer chez soi. La forme la plus pratique de conserver des verres consiste à les renverser et à les suspendre par la base. Pour ce faire, un bon porte-verres en bois ou en métal parallèle au reste des ustensiles est idéal.

EINE VOLLSTÄNDIGE BAR mit Theke, Spülbecken und Staumöbeln ist eine Fantasie vieler Personen. Das liegt daran, dass es das Bild eines intimen Ambientes, das im Haus genossen werden kann, erweckt. Die einfachste Art Weingläser aufzubewahren, ist kopfüber, an ihrem Boden aufgehängt. Um eine gute Halterung für die Weingläser zu schaffen, sind Holzleisten, die man parallell an den Regalen anbringt, praktisch.

console tables
consolas
consoles
konsolen

CONSOLE TABLES ARE VERY USEFUL for keeping or placing objects on top. Their benefits are that they are highly decorative and take up little space, because their depth is limited. They are usually set against the wall or next to the sofa. Originally, they were tall, narrow and long tables without doors, but today the term even extends to furniture with drawers.

LAS CONSOLAS SON ELEMENTOS ÚTILES para guardar o para colocar objetos encima de ellos. Tienen la ventaja de ser muy decorativas y ocupar poco espacio, pues son poco profundas. Por lo común se les ubica adosadas a muro o como respaldo de algún sofá. Originalmente eran mesas altas, estrechas, alargadas y sin puertas, pero hoy en día se ha extendido el término incluso para muebles con cajoneras.

LES CONSOLES SONT TRÈS UTILES pour ranger des choses ou pour placer dessus des objets. Très décoratives, elles présentent l'avantage d'occuper une place restreinte parce qu'elles sont peu profondes. On les adosse, en général, contre un mur ou elles font office de dossier pour un siège quelconque. À l'origine, les consoles étaient des tables hautes, étroites, allongées et sans portes aucune. À l'heure actuelle, la définition de ce terme s'est étoffée et on utilise même ce mot pour parler de meubles à tiroirs.

KONSOLEN SIND PRAKTISCHE MÖBEL zum Verstauen oder um auf ihnen Dinge aufzustellen. Sie haben den Vorteil, dass sie sehr dekorativ sind und wenig Platz wegnehmen, da sie nicht sehr tief sind. Normalerweise werden sie an die Wand angebettet oder am Rücken eines Sofas platziert. Ursprünglich waren sie hohe Tische, gerade, länglich und ohne Türen, aber heutzutage dehnt sich der Begriff sogar auf Möbel mit Schubladen aus.

IN ENTRANCE HALLS, HALLWAYS AND CORRIDORS, a console table may take on numerous roles, especially if it has a lot of drawers. Drawers are very practical for storing papers, mail, board games, keys, sewing implements and certain tools. If it is big and bulky, its visual presence can be toned down by placing some sizeable vases or candle holders on top of it, or even hanging items from the wall.

EN EL RECIBIDOR, EL VESTÍBULO Y EN ZONAS DE CIRCULACIÓN, una consola puede convertirse en un componente multifuncional, sobre todo si tiene numerosos cajones; éstos son muy prácticos para acopiar papeles, correo, juegos de mesa, llaves, notas, costureros y hasta algunas herramientas. Si el mueble es voluminoso, es factible nivelar su peso visual ubicando sobre él floreros o candelabros de buena dimensión y hasta piezas colgadas a la pared.

DANS L'ENTRÉE, DANS LE HALL OU DANS LES ZONES DE PASSAGE, une console peut servir à de multiples fonctions, surtout si elle comporte un grand nombre de tiroirs. En effet, ces derniers sont très pratiques pour y ranger des papiers, du courrier, des jeux de société, des clés, des notes, du matériel de couture, voire même quelques outils. Lorsque la console est volumineuse, il est possible d'atténuer son apparence en plaçant dessus des vases, des chandeliers de grande taille ou d'accrocher un tableau au mur.

IM EINGANGSBEREICH, DER DIELE ODER IN FLUREN kann sich eine Konsole in ein multifunktionelles Stück verwandeln, besonders wenn sie viele Schubladen hat; diese sind sehr praktisch um Papiere, Briefe, Brettspiele, Schlüssel, Notizen, Nähzeug und sogar einiges Werkzeug, unterzubringen. Wenn das Möbel gross ist, sollte sein optisches Gewicht durch Vasen oder Kerzenständer guter Grösse, oder Wandschmuck ausgeglichen werden.

IN A STUDY A CONSOLE TABLE CAN BE USED as a work corner that blends in with the rest of the room. Alternatively, it can be used to create an elegant and decorative space in tune with the room's overall balance and look. If it has drawers at the bottom, they should be large and deep so they can perform the role of a filing cabinet.

EN EL ESTUDIO, UNA CONSOLA FUNCIONA BIEN para conformar un rincón de trabajo que armonice con el conjunto; o bien para generar un espacio elegante y decorativo acorde con el equilibrio y la estética de la habitación. Si cuenta con cajoneras inferiores, que sean amplias y profundas, éstas pueden hacer las veces de archiveros.

DANS UN BUREAU, UNE CONSOLE sert à aménager un espace de travail qui s'intègre bien à l'ensemble. On peut aussi l'utiliser afin de créer un espace élégant et décoratif qui participera à l'équilibre et à l'esthétique de la pièce. Munie de tiroirs amples et profonds dans sa partie basse, elle peut même faire office de meubles pour y conserver des archives.

IM ARBEITSZIMMER HILFT EINE KONSOLE eine Arbeitsecke zu bilden, die mit dem Gesamten harmoniert; oder auch um einen eleganten und dekorativen Bereich in Einklang mit dem Gleichgewicht und der Ästhetik des Raumes zu schaffen. Wenn sie im unteren Teil Schubladen hat, können sie, wenn sie gross und tief sind, als Archivschrank genutzt werden.

A simple console table made with simple lines and right angles acquires an ornamental allure if plant pots or vases are added to the equation. It is also a light piece of furniture that can be moved from one place to another very easily.

Una consola sencilla, de líneas simples y ángulos rectos, luce como una pieza decorativa si se le añaden unas macetas o floreros. Además, es un mueble que por su ligereza se puede desplazar con facilidad de un sitio a otro.

Une console élémentaire, de lignes simples et à angles droits, prend l'apparence d'un objet décoratif si on la complète avec quelques pots de fleurs ou vases. Qui plus est, ce meuble, parce qu'il est léger, peut être facilement déplacé d'un endroit à un autre.

Eine einfache Konsole, mit schlichten Linien und rechten Winkeln, wird zu einem sehr dekorativen Möbel, wenn man auf ihr einige Blumentöpfe oder Vasen aufstellt. Ausserdem ist es ein Möbelstück, das sich durch seine Leichtigkeit einfach umstellen lässt.

A CONSOLE TABLE CAN ALSO BECOME AN AUXILIARY ITEM of furniture if it has panels for placing books along with a few decorative objects. However simple it may be, it helps dress the room and create a comfortable and functional setting. Its color, finish and style should tie in with the overall scheme.

LA CONSOLA TAMBIÉN SE VUELVE MOBILIARIO AUXILIAR si cuenta con entrepaños en medio en donde se puedan situar algunos libros compartiendo el espacio con otros elementos de ornato. Es un mueble que, por sencillo que sea, ayuda a vestir la habitación y a crear un espacio confortable y funcional; conviene, sin embargo, que su color, acabado y estilo estén vinculados con la composición general.

UNE CONSOLE PEUT FAIRE OFFICE DE MEUBLE D'APPOINT si elle est dotée de quelques étagères au milieu où l'on pourra placer quelques livres et elle s'ajoutera ainsi aux autres éléments de la décoration. Bien que simple, une console contribue à habiller une pièce et dote cette dernière d'un espace fonctionnel et confortable. Il est toutefois important que sa couleur, ses finitions et son style ne jurent pas dans l'atmosphère générale.

DIE KONSOLE WIRD AUCH zu einem nützlichen Möbelstück, wenn sie Zwischenböden in der Mitte aufweist, auf denen sich einige Bücher zusammen mit anderen Ziergegenständen ablegen lassen. Sie ist ein Möbel, so einfach es auch sein mag, dass hilft den Raum einzurichten und einen gemütlichen und funktionellen Bereich zu schaffen; sie sollte sich jedoch in ihrer Farbe, Verarbeitung und Stil in die Gesamtkompostion einfügen.

Modulation and symmetry determine the flow of a space. Such a balance is crucial if the storage furniture is large and spans the full length of the wall.

La modulación y la simetría marcan un ritmo en el espacio. Este equilibrio es determinante cuando un mueble de guardado posee dimensiones generosas y su longitud abarca el muro.

L'aspect multi-usuel et la symétrie d'un espace définissent son rythme. Cet équilibre est déterminant avec un meuble de rangement de taille imposante et dont la longueur couvre tout le mur.

Form und Symmetrie geben dem Raum Rhythmus. Dieses Gleichgewicht ist entscheidend, wenn ein Staumöbel sehr gross ist und seine Länge über die gesamte Wand reicht.

architecture arquitectónicos architectoniques architekten

96-97 *architectural project:* A-001 TALLER DE ARQUITECTURA, eduardo gorozpe

98-99 *interior design project:* EZEQUIEL FARCA, ezequiel farca

101 *interior design project:* JSª, javier sánchez y pola zaga

108-109 *architectural project:* GGAD, gerardo garcía l.

110 *architectural project:* BERNARDO HINOJOSA, bernardo hinojosa ruíz, *interior design project:* martha elizondo de sada, *contributors:* aurora delgado, jaime ávila, hiram pruneda, lauro villarreal

116-117 *interior design project:* ARCO ARQUITECTURA CONTEMPORÁNEA, josé lew y bernardo lew, *contributors:* oscar sarabia, jonathan herrejón, miguel ocampo, yuritza gonzález, itzel ortiz, nahela hinojosa, gabriela pineda, guillermo martínez, federico teista, martha tenopala y beatriz canuto

118-119 *architectural project:* ANONIMOUS-LED, alfonso jiménez, marco a. velázquez, jorge plascencia, vittorio bonetti, ricardo martínez, cesar medina y roberto ramírez

122 *interior design project:* OLIMPIC KITCHEN AND FURNITURE COLLECTION

124-125 *architectural project:* LASSALA + ELENES, carlos lassala m., eduardo lassala m., diego mora d., guillermo r. orozco y o.

126-127 *architectural project:* GA GRUPO ARQUITECTURA, daniel álvarez fernández, *contributors:* rosa lópez, susana lópez y raúl chávez

128-129 *architectural project:* CENTRAL DE ARQUITECTURA, josé sánchez y moisés isón, *interior design project:* moisés isón, *contributors:* alejandro juárez herrera, nicolás vázquez herrmann y carlos del monte bergés

130-131 *architectural project:* GA GRUPO ARQUITECTURA, daniel álvarez fernández, *contributors:* héctor ferral, susana lópez y rosa lópez

132-133 *architectural project:* RDLP, rodrigo de la peña l., *contributors:* mauricio maycotte, nora nelly zamarrón

134 *interior design project:* TEXTURA®, walter allen, *architectural project:* jacobo gudiño, *contributors:* paolo rindone

142-143 *architectural project:* AGRAZ ARQUITECTOS, ricardo agraz, *contributors:* alberto tacher, sara tamez, efraín aguirre, jessica magaña, marisol reynoso, erick martínez y javier gutiérrez

148-149 *architectural project:* LASSALA + ELENES, carlos lassala m., eduardo lassala m., diego mora d., guillermo r. orozco y o.

156 *architectural and interior design project:* GGAD, gerardo garcía l.

158-159 *architectural project:* DI VECE Y ASOCIADOS, paolino di vece roux, *interior design project:* bricio fernández

160-161 *interior design project:* OLIMPIC KITCHEN AND FURNITURE COLLECTION

167 *architectural and interior design project:* ABAX, fernando de haro, jesús fernández, omar fuentes y bertha figueroa

169 *architectural project:* MICHEAS ARQUITECTOS, antonio micheas vázquez, *contributors:* diego armando cano gonzález, fernando jiménez hernández y miguel angel izquierdo avilés

178 *interior design project:* OLIMPIC KITCHEN AND FURNITURE COLLECTION

186-187 *interior design project:* OLIMPIC KITCHEN AND FURNITURE COLLECTION

188-189 *architectural and interior design project:* ABAX, fernando de haro, jesús fernández, omar fuentes y bertha figueroa

architecture arquitectónicos architectoniques architekten

photography fotográficos photographiques fotografen

adrian montes - pg. 193 (bottom)

arturo chávez - pgs. 44-45, 58 (top), 72-73, 230, 238-239, 250, 254-255

© beta-plus publishing - pgs. 4-5, 10-11, 14-15, 31, 34-41, 52-57, 62-71, 76-78, 88-95, 102-106, 112-115, 120-121, 136-141, 145-146, 150-155, 162-165, 168, 170-177, 180-185, 190-191, 196, 199-201, 208-215, 219 (top and bottom), 232-233, 244-245, 248-249

carlos soto - pg. 134

francisco lubbert - pg. 110

gabriela ibarra - pg. 207

gerardo garcía l. - pgs. 3, 108-109

guadalupe castillo - pg. 207

héctor flora - pg. 134

héctor velasco facio - pgs. 9, 17-21, 30, 46-47, 82-83, 156, 198, 204-205, 216-217, 228-229, 241

jaime navarro - pgs. 32-33, 48-51, 59, 98-99, 116-117, 193 (top), 202-203, 226, 235

jorge rodríguez almanza - pgs. 219 (right), 220

jorge taboada - pgs. 132-133

luis gordoa - pgs. 22-23, 126-127

marcos garcía - pgs. 124-125, 148-149

maría fernanda olivieri san giacomo - pg. 242

maría isabel santaularia - pgs. 96-97

manuel garcía - pgs. 96-97

mark callanan - pgs. 28-29, 60-61, 80-81, 84-86, 167, 188-189, 222-225, 260-261

mike paz y puente - pgs. 236-237

mito covarrubias - pgs. 142-143, 158-159

nancy ambe - pg. 134

olimpic kitchen and furniture collection - pgs. 122, 160-161, 178, 186-187, 194-195

paul czitrom - pgs. 24-27, 58 (bottom), 75, 128-131, 192, 252-253

pim schalkwijk - pg. 101

ricardo janet - pgs. 8, 118-119

verónica areli martínez paz - pgs. 246-247

víctor benítez - pg. 169

Editado en Junio 2010. Impreso en China. El cuidado de
esta edición estuvo a cargo de AM Editores, S.A. de C.V.
Edited in June 2010. Printed in China. Published by
AM Editores, S.A. de C.V.